C000093784

You Don't Need Money, You Just Need God

A PLAYBOOK FOR MIRACULOUS PROVISION

Jaime Luce
with Judy Mercer

TRILOGY CHRISTIAN PUBLISHERS

TUSTIN, CA

Trilogy Christian Publishers
A Wholly Owned Subsidary of Trinity Broadcasting Network
2442 Michelle Drive
Tustin, CA 92780

You Don't Need Money, You Just Need God

For information, address Trilogy Christian Publishing

Rights Department, 2442 Michelle Drive, Tustin, CA 92780.

Trilogy Christian Publishing/ TBN and colophon are trademarks of Trinity Broadcasting Network.

For information about special discounts for bulk purchases, please contact Trilogy Christian Publishing.

Manufactured in the United States of America

10 9 8 7 6 5 4 3 2 1

Library of Congress Cataloging-in-Publication Data is available.

ISBN: 978-1-68556-474-2

ISBN: 978-1-68556-475-9

Dedication

I want to dedicate this book first to the Lord who saw fit to use the *least of these* to share His unfailing and enduring message. He has blessed me more than I could have thought or imagined. His word has proved true, constant, and available in every situation, and I am eternally grateful for His gift. Second, to my husband and the love of my life, Joel. If it were not for his belief in me, his constant encouragement, and his provision over my life, this could never have been possible. Third, to my mother, Judy. Her tutelage and hunger for the Word of God continue to teach and inspire the same love and appetite in me.

Introduction

Jaime Luce

Have you ever stared at a bill so long your eyes hurt, all because you had no way to pay it? Or maybe you've lost your job and at the worst possible time? Maybe you've got a deep longing to start that business but there is absolutely no money, and the banks won't give you the loan? You need a home. Or worse yet, you could lose your home. Let me encourage you. You don't have to be afraid of whatever is standing in front of you, taunting you like Goliath did to David! In the pages that follow, you, like David, will find the stones for your sling that will bring that giant down.

All of us at one time or another have had seemingly insurmountable financial needs. You're not alone. But knowing what to do while you're facing great need is critical. The beauty of the answer to this problem is that it can be used over and over again and for any size financial need. Though my mother saw the principle modeled for her, the revelation of it was found one quiet morning.

She was sitting in her chair surrounded by piles of books and papers and with her pen and highlighter in hand, doing what she did most days. Studying the Bible for her next message was and is her constant labor of love. She is like a treasure hunter gathering all her tools while studying her map intently. The passages are so familiar, yet each time they are read, they are seen with fresh eyes.

On this day, the hunt is on and somehow the story seems different. Then, all of a sudden, she sees something being unearthed as it catches the light. It's the glimmer of something gold. Could it be that a new nugget has just been found? No. Not this time. This time it isn't just a nugget. It's an entire treasure!

She didn't know it then, but this treasure would change everything. What she found that day she would need over and over again. This *treasure of truth* would become the inheritance that she would pass to her children, and they would pass to theirs.

Jesus told the parable in Matthew 13:44 *"The Kingdom of heaven is like a treasure hidden in a field. When a man found it, he hid it again, and then in his joy went and sold all he had and bought that field"* (NIV).

What treasure could she possibly have found that would change how we live and demand that we share it with you? What is this secret unearthed? It is this. *You don't need money. You just need God.* It is so powerfully true that when laid hold of it produces an audacious faith! She said, *"It can seem like a pretty absurd concept initially.... You don't need money?"* WHAT? What planet do I live on? I remember hearing, "money is like oxygen; you can't live without it, or money makes the world go 'round."

Let me explain. In the book of John, Jesus performed the miracle of feeding the 5,000. And that was just the men! Some Bible scholars have estimated that "if you also include women and children, the total fed that day was closer to 20,000. Twenty thousand people! According to Philip, financially it was impossible. What Jesus fed them with that day was a meager sack lunch of five barley cakes and two small fish made for a little boy, yet they had twelve baskets full left over.

Now if God can feed 20,000 people with a little sack lunch, then what could He do for you?

As a pastor, teacher, and co-founder of a successful church plant, my mother imparted and lived the principles of scripture, which was and is her life's calling. She has victoriously maneuvered countless financial hurdles. For over fifty years, she has faithfully taught thousands an unshakeable faith while scaling the hurdles of needs, both at home and at church, with less than a sack lunch. And she watched God do the impossible every time. She continues to fill her days encouraging and equipping others to dare to put their trust in God with truth and authority regardless of the circumstance they find themselves in, knowing that God cannot fail.

This same truth has been the platform my husband and I have jumped off every time we've needed provision. Being business owners of two successful companies, we have deployed this book's powerful truth again and again. It has been the backbone at every critical financial juncture for home and business for more than twenty-five years. During that time, I have had the pleasure of teaching, pastoring, podcasting, and blogging about the treasures found in the Word of God. And now it's your turn. I am passing this baton to you, giving you the tools to run your specific race.

It really doesn't matter how large or how small your need is. When you don't have the means, you need God's intervention. He has never failed to fulfill every deficit we have faced whether in our personal lives or our ministry lives. And since He is no respecter of persons, He will do the same for you. That is why this book is so important.

Our desire in writing this for you is to dispel the lie that if you don't have money then it's impossible to do what you need to do. Nothing is impossible with God! In fact, the opposite is true. All things are possible! And we can show you how.

In a court of law there is a burden of proof. Our lives have put this truth on trial. We have written this to put into evidence the facts as we lived them. We want to erase all reasonable doubt that you may have in believing that God isn't big enough for your need. We can promise that once you have read this book, the evidence will show that He is greater. Much greater. The gavel can come down pronouncing that He is able to do exceedingly and abundantly more than you could ask or imagine.

This is not a "name it and claim it" or ten steps to financial freedom handbook. This is a playbook. Playbooks are used to guide which plays you can deploy when facing an opponent. Even the fans of an opposing team understand this concept. Their hope is to cheer so loudly as to distract and actually impact the game. Their interference of noise can not only make it difficult to hear but to also affect momentum. The right decisions made in faith will always create a momentum of favor in your life. Knowing the plays will make all the difference.

Contained in these pages are the stories detailing our family's playbook for financial success. They tell you how we fought our battles and won. Your opponent the devil is sly. He will try to confuse the play and distract you so you can't hear the play-call. There's no need to be fooled. Written in this book is your new play call. Focus in and listen well. You don't need money. You just need God.

Multiple benefits are found in every chapter. You'll get an inside look at the details of those needs you may be facing, and the steps we used to practically walk them out. You'll be given the biblical perspective in scriptures and lessons that will teach and explain the heart of God and how He moves on behalf of those who seek Him. These lessons will teach you how God sees your situation and what adjustments you may need to make so that you can claim a victory where there seemed to be a defeat.

What you learn will prove to be a weapon you can wield whenever you need it. You can take each lesson learned and share them with your children in order to bring freedom from lack and overcome the impossible. You will possess a treasure that never loses its value, a true inheritance. You will see for yourselves how we didn't need money. We just needed God. And the same will be said for you!

At the end of each chapter, you will find a focused prayer. We encourage you to find a place where you can regularly meet with the Lord for prayer. Our desire is that these prayers will be the beginning of a more extended time of talking with your Heavenly Father. They will help you begin your prayer and to set your heart on Him in order to focus on what you really need.

From the beginning, God showed us in Genesis His desire to be in daily communion with us. He never expected us to live this life alone. He never intended for us be in lack. In His love for us, He created a garden first and then put the man in it, teaching us that he would prepare for our needs ahead of time. In every place He calls you, you can know that He has already planned the provision and made preparation. His desire was and still is to make this journey together.

Whether you need this revelation for yourself, your family, your business, or you are actively involved in ministry and are navigating the needs of the church, you will find His guidance on the pages of this book.

Walking with Jesus is a wonder-filled journey where everything you ever need, He becomes. This is why He calls himself the "I AM." He is excited for you to come and follow Him just as His disciples did. He loves to teach and to lead and He longs to feed your hunger, physically, emotionally, and spiritually.

Don't wait any longer. Don't delay taking the journey of following Jesus. It's time to get out the treasure map and start digging. You won't be disappointed.

You Don't Need Money. You Just Need God.

Contents

"I love this book...I found the stories very uplifting and very inspiring...I recommend it...and I encourage people to read it."

Jack Canfield
American author, motivational speaker,
corporate trainer, and entrepreneur
(Co-Author of *Chicken Soup for the Soul* series)

"I've known Jaime Luce now for many years. I've had a front row seat as she and her husband navigated the turbulent waters of entrepreneurship since 2007. I've been involved at a level that I got to see it all miraculously happen. Jaime is a God-fearing, God-centered lady, who believes deeply in prayer and the Word. This is a glimpse from the other side of entrepreneurship, from the wife's perspective, but her rendition is spot on I must say. What a great resource for anyone who's spouse is passionate about their business, and deeply passionate about their God, but still living in this turbulent world. Excellent read!"

Galen Walters
CEO/Chairman Relationshop Inc.,
Author, teacher, leadership coach, and
businessman.

"I am delighted to recommend this book to one and all because we have all experienced financial need and often have found ourselves at the proverbial end of our rope. This practical guide for depending upon God to meet our needs is Bible-based and filled with personal experiences that bring it to life and make it applicable to our lives. The personal stories will keep the reader riveted and engaged. And of the many memorable tips and principles so succinctly presented, I find this one the most encouraging: "… If It Matters to You, It Matters to God." I'm always amazed how God answers even the seemingly insignificant requests I make to God, such as asking him to help me find my car keys or glasses. It's absolutely true, that if it matters to you, it matters to God! And it matters to God that we are reminded through this wonderful book how faithful he is to meet our needs."

Mitch Land, PhD
Professor, Dean of Media and Worship Arts,
The King's University

"I have been blessed to watch Jaime and her husband Joel genuinely live their life pursuing the Kingdom of God in all areas. Jaime has such a sincere love for the Lord, and her experiences in business and life have thoroughly equipped her ability to impact others in a profound way through her story and insights. Not only will this book bless you, but it will equip and empower you to live your life in a way that will bless others."

Ps Ben Prescott
Lead Pastor, Free Chapel Orange County

CHAPTER 1

The Key to Provision

Judy Mercer

As my sleepy, blurry eyes peeped open, I slowly made my way down the winding staircase. The smell of fresh-brewed coffee from my pre-set coffee maker enticed me into the morning. Out of sheer habit I poured myself a cup and filled my coffee carafe. Quietly, I made my way to my favorite spot in the family room. With that always present, deep yearning for God, I automatically picked up my Bible. Like an athlete in daily disciplined training to hone my skills, this was my daily pursuit. Little did I realize that the Holy Spirit was about to plant a powerful seed in me that morning. A seed that would grow to such a magnitude, that our whole family would taste of its fruit for years to come.

As I read the Gospel of John, Jesus was miraculously feeding the 5,000. And that was just the men. Some Bible scholars have estimated that if you also included women and children, the total fed that day was closer to 20,000 people. All fed from a little boy's humble lunch. But something piqued my curiosity. The scripture states that Jesus gave Philip a test that preempted this miracle. We're told Jesus ALREADY KNEW HOW He would meet this need. Why test Philip? Why was the test necessary? What was the test designed to reveal?

Jesus queried Philip. Where would they get food to feed this massive crowd? It was Philip's response that cut like a knife into my heart. His answer was so quick, so normal, so rational, and so just like me! His mind automatically went to the *money*. The *amount* of money they would need. Philip, being overwhelmed by *how much money* it would take, says 200 denarii wouldn't be enough to give them even a taste! In Philip's day 200 denarii would equate to roughly eight months' wages. He had already resigned himself to the brutal fact. *It is impossible*. We just don't have the money!

As the miracle unfolds, Jesus's other disciple, Andrew, is also assessing the impossibility they faced. He blurts out that there is a little boy in the crowd with a packed lunch of five little cakes and two small fish. Realizing how ridiculous that sounds, he fatalistically replies, how far would that go with this huge crowd? It seems like a dead-end. It can't be done. It's just impossible. But with our God *nothing* is impossible! He is Almighty God. The God of more-than-enough. Jesus takes that little boy's lunch into His hands, looks up into heaven, blesses it and WHALA! The scriptures say they *all* ate. And they were all *filled*. There were even twelve baskets of leftovers! Like someone switching on a giant floodlight, the revelation overwhelmed me – YOU DON'T NEED MONEY. YOU JUST NEED GOD.

In that moment, my mind went back to a man's testimony from years before. He felt he was to make a gospel album. In researching, he discovered he would need $15,000 for studio time (*I said it was years ago*). Since he didn't have $15,000, he began praying and praying for God to provide the $15,000 he needed. Day after day, week after week, he continued to pray, "Lord, I need $15,000." "Lord, please, provide the $15,000." But no money was materializing. One day, he received a call from a man he didn't know. The man said he had heard about his desire to make a gospel album. The man went on to say, "Well, I just happen to own a recording studio, and I would like to donate all the studio time you need so you can make that album." There was the revelation again ... *You don't need money. You just need God.*

The scriptures are constantly reinforcing this truth to us. Acts chapter three gives the testimony of a man crippled from birth. He was carried every day to the entrance of the temple where he would beg for money. On seeing Peter and John going into the temple, he calls out to them, and they stop. When he sees they are looking at him, we read he expected a gift of money from them.

That's what he had been begging for. Money. But what happened next, he didn't expect. They told him they *didn't have ANY money*, but they did have what he really needed. Something they knew he needed more than money. Something that no amount of money could ever buy for him. Peter said, *"Silver and gold I do not have, but what I do have I give to you. In the name of Jesus Christ of Nazareth, rise up and walk!"* (NKJV). Peter reaches out his hand and lifts the crippled man up. Suddenly, power surged into his crippled feet and ankles. He begins jumping and shouting praises to God and walks into the temple with Peter and John!

The man wanting to make an album had so focused on *the money*, the $15,000, but that wasn't his real need! His *REAL NEED* was to make a gospel album. Philip had so focused on the 200 denarii but that wasn't his real need. His *REAL NEED* was food to feed the people. The man at the temple thought he needed money, but that wasn't his real need either. His *REAL NEED* was to be healed, so he would never have to beg again.

Somehow our minds always go first to the money. *If I just had the money....* If I just had the money to hire a good attorney. If I just had the money for the down payment. If I just had the money to go to school. If I just had the money to buy a new car. On and on our minds go at lightning speed. We're always feeling like money is our answer. The money will fix our problems. It would all happen for me if I just had the money. Emotionally, we can become like the high-speed greyhounds that are trained for dog races. High in the control tower someone is operating a mechanical electric rabbit, just beyond the dog's reach, and ever increasing the speed. It's the lure they chase but are never able to obtain. Money can be a lure we chase, and yet our real needs are never satisfied. The false chasing will run us ragged.

Yes, of course, we truly have many needs; real needs, tangible needs, monetary needs, emotional needs, relational needs, and spiritual needs, on and on. God knows *all* of our needs, and He is able to meet every need we as human beings have. And He wants to meet our needs. He is a good Father who loves to give good gifts to His kids! But our *real need* is God first! Matthew 16:26 reads *"For what will it profit a man if he gains the whole world and forfeits his soul?"* (ESV). In Matthew 6:33 we're told, *"But seek first the kingdom of God and His righteousness, and all these things will be added to you"* (NKJV).

PLAY CALL: *Identify the real need.*

The definition of *need* is something that is essential. Necessary. A requirement. Often, we don't recognize what our *real need* is... life can overwhelm us with so much. We can inadvertently find ourselves chasing that 'electric rabbit' that never really meets the need. We can easily focus on the wrong thing. Proverbs 16:25 reveals

"There is a path before each person that seems right, but it ends in death" (NLT). The answers will come when we turn to GOD FIRST. That, in reality, is *our real need.*

IDENTIFY THE REAL NEED
The Key to Provision

Principle 1: *God's Word.*

The Word of God is your source for knowing God and knowing your real needs. He has revealed Himself and everything He has purposed for your life in His written word. The more you are acquainted with the Bible, the more you will find the answers and the direction you seek. 1 Timothy 4:8 tells us, *"For while bodily training is of some value, godliness is of value in every way, as it holds promise for the present life and also for the life to come"* (ESV). 2 Peter 1:3 states, *"His divine power has granted to us all things that pertain to life and godliness, through the knowledge of Him who called us to His own glory and excellence"* (ESV). It is God's Word that enables you to stay focused on your real needs and then will guide you on the path to meeting those needs.

Principle 2: *Prayer.*

Once you've identified your need, you then bring that need to God in prayer. Praying to the Father in the name of Jesus, shows you are putting your faith in Him first. We are reminded in John 14:6 Jesus said to him, *"I am the way, and the truth, and the life. No one comes to the Father except through me"* (ESV). The Word is full of God's promises and when you pray, you declare your faith in those promises He has made. Philippians 4:6 says, *"Don't worry about anything; instead, pray about everything"* (NLT2). Tell God what you need and thank Him for all He has done.

God can and will meet your needs, with or without money. After all, Jesus is the miracle worker! He can turn water into wine! He can feed 5,000 men with a handful of food. He can sustain a widow woman by miraculously filling jars of oil that are then sold and thereby continue sustaining her during a famine. He can rain down manna from heaven and *he can meet your needs* if you recognize it's GOD YOU REALLY NEED!

The revelation that God gave me that early sleepy morning has become the foundation of our lives and the lives of our children. As I began to live this truth out, the events throughout our lives have demonstrated the miraculous power that is unleashed when you look to God first and you discover *you don't need money, you just need God!*

PRAYER

Lord, let the knowledge that I only need You, take root in my heart. You are the source of all that I need. Help me let go of the thoughts that lie to me and tell me it's impossible. Help me lay hold of the truth that through You, all things are possible. Give me the kind of faith that causes the faith in others to be stirred. I declare that I will see You do the miraculous in my life and the lives of my family. In Jesus's name, Amen.

CHAPTER 2

It's All in Who You Know

Judy Mercer

There I was with my two long, thick, brown-haired braids, parted right down the middle, looking just like Dorothy out of *The Wizard of Oz*. I was at the age where I was just beginning to become conscious that being popular was 'a thing.' Being in grade school it quickly became apparent to me that it was important to be liked, to fit-in, to be accepted and considered 'cool.' I was a quick study and I soon realized you needed to have a certain 'look'... the 'cool kids' dressed a certain way. Every recess we played hopscotch and the "cool girls' had taps put on their saddle-oxford shoes and with each hop, those shoes clicked! And THAT was 'cool' to everybody.

Because my father was out of our lives and my mother was a single parent in a two-parent world at that time, money was always scarce. This made it a big problem for me to be able to 'look the part' and gain the approval

I longed for at school. I felt so alone and helpless to be able to measure up. Little did I realize at that young age that God was about to teach me His wonderful truth: *You don't need money. You just need God.*

It all came to a crisis point one day. I had to go to my mom and say, "Mom, I really need some shoes." I pretty much had resigned myself to the fact that I might get some new bargain-basement shoes, but I would never be able to have the shoes I really wanted. My young heart passionately yearned for a pair of saddle-oxford shoes, with those taps, that was all the rage. Well, my mother's quick answer to me was, "Judy, you don't have an earthly father that can provide for you, but you have a Heavenly Father – you can go and ask your Heavenly Father for new shoes."

Well, that's exactly what I did. I was dead serious about getting those saddle-oxford shoes! If that was the only recourse I had, I would take it. I distinctly remember marching myself into the bedroom, kneeling down by the bed and earnestly praying to my Heavenly Father. "Dear God, I really, really need new shoes! Please will you provide them for me. I promise I will be so thankful to you if you do. Amen."

To this day I don't remember the details of *how* I got those shoes – I know my mom truly didn't have the money but miraculously from somewhere or someone shortly came the provision. The day I rushed into that shoe store and came out with my prized pair of Saddle-Oxford shoes, taps and all, *I KNEW God was REAL!* I knew He hears you when you pray – and He not only hears, He *ANSWERS!* All my young mind could think before was *we need money* but all I really needed was GOD! From that day onward, I have carried a confidence in me that you can turn to the Lord with the desires of your heart, and He loves and cares about you so personally that *if it matters to you, it matters to Him!*

PLAY CALL: *Bring the desires of your heart to God.*

In hindsight I now realize how wise my mother had been. How easily she could have made it all about *her...* she could have said, "Well, Judy, I will pray, and I will ask God for you," and she would have become my hero. But she wanted me to know God for myself. She wanted me to learn that you can bring your personal needs and the desires of your heart to the God whose love surpasses any earthly love we can ever know. She wanted me to experience as she had, that the true hero of our lives is GOD! Jesus Christ, the same yesterday, today, and forever! I would never again question that I had a Heavenly Father that was real. He had proved Himself to be my God and I could bring to Him all the longings of my heart. Do you need a Heavenly Father? Do you have desires that you long for deep in your heart? He is just a prayer away and He truly cares.

BRING THE DESIRES OF YOUR HEART TO GOD
It's All in Who You Know

Principle 1: *God Is Personal.*

We tend to make God merely religious. We place Him in rituals, observances, ceremonies, holidays, and stained glass. We identify Him with creation, or a church, a choir or a person's philosophy. He is viewed so often as far away, out of reach or even out of touch. In reality, God is our Father! How could God make it any more personal to us than that? OUR FATHER. That's exactly how Jesus taught us to pray. *"Pray then like this: Our Father in heaven, hallowed be Your name."* Matthew 6:9 (ESV). Notice how personal Jesus made it for us. 'Our father'... just as my mother had made Him personal to me. That's what Jesus has done for each of us. He has opened the door for us to know Him and come to Him on the basis of being His child. A father whose love and goodness towards us can never be exhausted. It is through the individual needs of our lives that He reveals to us the depth of His care and concern for us personally.

Principle 2: *If It Matters to You, It Matters to God.*

The Psalmist himself declared in Psalms 138:8, *"The Lord will perfect that which concerns me; Your mercy and lov-ing-kindness, O Lord, endure forever—forsake not the works of Your own hands"* (AMP). King David knew God on a deep, personal level. He had experienced God helping him in a multitude of situations throughout his life. God had time and time again shown to him that whatever mattered to him, mattered to His God as well.

We find this truth throughout the entire Bible. Situation after situation, need after need, plea after plea, the Lord God showed Himself caring and faithful to the needs and petitions of His children. We read in 1 Samuel, chapters one and two of a woman's passionate desire to have a baby. It doesn't get any more personal than that. With every passing year, her emptiness and yearning only intensified. It didn't seem to matter to anyone else, not even her husband, who thought she was making way too big of a deal about it. But it so mattered to Hannah, and everything changed when Hannah brought it to the Lord. 1 Samuel 1:10... *"And she was bitter, and prayed to the Lord, and wept severely."* From that moment on things began to change. Verse 20 says, *"And in due time Hannah conceived and bore a son, and she called his name Samuel, for she said, 'I have asked for him from the LORD'"* (ESV). Hannah was to learn that if it mattered to her, it also mattered to God. She brought what mattered to her to the God who hears and answers. 1 Samuel 1:27 - *For this child I prayed, and the LORD has granted me my petition that I made to Him* (ESV).

I can't help but wonder how many things we could see birthed in our lives if we would lay hold of this truth for ourselves. Matthew 6:6, *But when you pray, go into your room, and shut the door and pray to your Father who is in secret. And your Father who sees in secret will reward you* (ESV). Don't carry any barrenness anymore in any area of your life. Whatever matters to you, you have the assurance, it also matters to your God.

I've come a long way since my days of long braids and Saddle-Oxford shoes. But that truth that God imparted to me as a young girl, has shaped my walk with God and transformed my relationship with my heavenly Father. The multitude of miracles I've experienced for myself, and my family have all come about because I learned from an early age *you don't need money. You just need God!*

PRAYER

Lord, you have promised that you would meet our needs no matter how large or how small. Thank you for allowing me to come boldly to your throne room of grace and make my petitions known to you. Help me to wait patiently on your generosity knowing that you know my need even before I ask. I will trust you because you are always a good Father, and you care about what concerns me. In Jesus's name, Amen.

CHAPTER 3

When You're Down to Your Last Dollar

Jaime Luce

With tears streaming down my face, I sat with my head bowed while our pastor prayed over the offering. "This is all I have but it belongs to you," I uttered in prayer. I had exactly thirty-five dollars and that is exactly what I owed in tithe. I knew what I needed to do. I had always tithed. Even as a little girl I would tithe even my birthday money. But this time it hurt. This time I was the one in need.

My mind went through the options. Maybe I can give next time. God knows this is all I have. I could just give a few dollars until my next paycheck. I've given for all these years. Does this time really matter? I'm responsible to feed my children. Doesn't God know that?

I was a newly single mother of two children. I was the one working a job that was fifty miles from my parents' home where I was staying. The emotional and physical strain was overwhelming most days, but I had no other choice but to keep putting one foot in front of the other. The babies still needed to be fed, and the bills still needed to be paid. But I couldn't run from what I knew. With trembling hands, I obeyed the Lord. I wrote the check and placed it in the offering plate.

That thirty-five dollars was all I had to pay my car insurance, buy diapers, and baby food, and put gas in my car. It wasn't even enough to do that but giving it meant I'd have nothing. I was completely undone.

This journey I was now on was one of complete reliance on the God I called mine. I said I believed in Him. I said we have to live by faith. Well, it's a lot easier to say that when you don't need anything. My faith had to go from a head faith to a life surrendered faith. There is a big difference. People say faith is stepping out onto nothing but landing on something. On this night, I was literally looking over the cliff with the rocks slipping off the edge under my feet and into the abyss. This was a defining moment. Tonight, I closed my eyes in prayer and stepped off the ledge.

The rest of the night was an internal panic. I tried to come up with an idea or see something that maybe I missed. How can I get to work tomorrow with no gas in the car? What am I going to do? I racked my brain to no avail and finally fell to sleep out of sheer emotional exhaustion.

I woke up the next morning in a fog and got dressed for work. I don't know what I was thinking since I had no way to get there. I was just numb and going through the motions. I couldn't face that I didn't have a way to fix this. As I walked to the garage door to go to my car, I heard my mother who had just come downstairs. Still half asleep she said, "Jaime, wait a minute. I almost forgot. Last night at church, a woman who wants to remain anonymous came up to me and said that while she sat in service, the Lord spoke to her and told her to give this to you." I said, "What? Really?" My mom handed me the folded paper. I opened it up. I couldn't believe it. It was $100.00. I immediately began to cry. It was exactly enough to get gas, pay my insurance and buy the diapers and formula I needed. He loved me in that moment of pain and need, more than anyone can ever know, and I will forever love Him for it.

I know the moment I gave God what was rightfully His, He spoke to that woman on my behalf. At that very moment an exchange was made. We'd sealed the contract. I did what was required of me and He did exactly what He said He would do.

It was the moment I went from hoping God's promises are true to knowing they are. It was the day I had sacrificed all that I had to obey, and He was watching. And it was the day I learned for myself that *You don't need money. You just need God.*

PLAY CALL: *Bring your finances into Covenant with God.*

I had "some" money. I could have thought to hang onto the money supposing it was the answer. Jesus said to *"render unto Cesar the things that are Cesar's and render to God the things that are God's"* (Mark 12:17, ASV). I didn't have enough money. What I needed was God. I needed him to make what little I had become enough.

TITHING
When You're Down to Your Last Dollar

The fascinating thing is that it isn't just my story. This happens every day for those who are in covenant with the Lord in regard to their finances. The Bible speaks about tithing and giving throughout. It is one of the simplest things we can do to change our current financial status. It's cut and dry. No special hoops to jump through. God says if we will give Him what rightfully belongs to Him, He will in turn watch over what you have, multiply it, and not allow it to be robbed by outside forces.

For instance, you just save enough to finally make a purchase or pay a bill or put a little in savings, and the dishwasher breaks down or you run over a nail and have to replace the tire. Scripture describes it like this in Haggai 1:6: *"You have planted much, but harvested little. You eat, but never have enough. You drink, but never have your fill. You put on clothes, but are not warm. You earn wages, only to put them in a purse with holes in it"* (NIV).

The reason this happens many times is simply the lack of tithing. It is not because God is demanding or that He even needs your money. He doesn't. What He needs is for you to come into agreement with Him to bless you. I don't get the privilege of calling Joel Luce my husband simply by meeting him. I took a vow and made a covenant with him. What I had became his, and what he had became mine. In the same way, I am not in covenant with God simply because I believe He is there. I must come into a covenant relationship with him. In essence, I marry him. Our finances are now tied together. What I have becomes his, and what he has becomes mine. It doesn't matter if I have only meager means since he owns it all. Through Him I now have access to all I need. So then as a Christian, this is why he considers it robbery to not tithe. A covenant is not one sided. It's a joint agreement like a marriage. Each agrees to the vows of the covenant.

In business loans and investments, banks will have "covenants." You must meet the expectation of your agreement. In other words, you must not break the covenants or there are penalties you incur. You could even end up losing your shares. It is the same with God. He is your bank. He owns it all. Scripture tells us in Haggai 2:8 *"The silver is mine, and the gold is mine, saith the Lord of hosts"* (KJV). He also says in Psalms 24:1 that *"The earth is the LORD's, and all its fullness, the world and those who dwell therein"* (NKJV). It all belongs to Him.

I'll give you an example. If I hand you a hundred-dollar bill and then ask you to give it to me, you are not giving me a hundred dollars. You are returning to me my hundred dollars. This is tithing. God is not even asking for all of it back. He simply asks for ten percent. The word tithe literally means "the tenth." We give the first tenth, and God blesses the ninety percent. In essence, He uses only ten percent to care for your one hundred percent.

So, what exactly does scripture say about tithing? I'm glad you asked. Malachi 3:7-12 says this:

> [7] *Ever since the time of your ancestors you have turned away from my decrees and have not kept them. Return to me, and I will return to you," says the Lord Almighty. "But you ask, 'How are we to return?' [8] "Will a mere mortal rob God? Yet you rob Me. "But you ask, 'How are we robbing you?' "In tithes and offerings. [9] You are under a curse— your whole nation—because you are robbing Me. [10]Bring the whole tithe into the storehouse, that there may be food in My house. Test me in this," says the Lord Almighty, "and see if I will not throw open the floodgates of heaven and pour out so much blessing that there will not be room enough to store it. [11] I will prevent pests from devouring your crops, and the vines in your fields will not drop their fruit before it is ripe," says the Lord Almighty. [12] "Then all*

*the nations will call you blessed, for yours will be a
delightful land," says the Lord Almighty.* (NIV)

Not only does God consider not tithing robbery, but
it's a curse. Meaning, your finances are not blessed.
Quite the opposite. Without being in covenant you are
like a city without walls. You will have no protection
from the robbery of the enemy. That's why the refrig-
erator went out and the car broke down. There is no
protection over your wealth. God is not being mean. He
just has no jurisdiction over something that you won't
put Him in charge of. John 10:10 says that *"The thief does
not come except to steal, and to kill, and to destroy. I have come
that they may have life, and that they may have it more abundantly"* (NKJV). The enemy will curse what you have but
God will give life to all you have.

The passage we highlighted in Malachi has three
principles of tithing. To walk in them will bring blessing back upon your finances:

> *10 Bring the whole tithe into the storehouse, that
> there may be food in My house. Test me in this,"
> says the Lord Almighty, "and see if I will not throw
> open the floodgates of heaven and pour out so much
> blessing that there will not be room enough to store
> it. 11 I will prevent pests from devouring your crops,
> and the vines in your fields will not drop their fruit
> before it is ripe," says the Lord Almighty* (NIV).

Let's break them down.

Principle 1: *Bring the whole tithe.*

It says the whole tithe. Many will say they give in the offering at church. How much and how often depends on how much they have and how much they want to give and when they want to give it. This was the mistake that Cain made which led to envy and murder:

Genesis 4:2-7:

> *²Now Abel kept flocks, and Cain worked the soil. ³In the course of time Cain brought some of the fruits of the soil as an offering to the Lord. ⁴ And Abel also brought an offering—fat portions from some of the firstborn of his flock. The Lord looked with favor on Abel and his offering, ⁵ but on Cain and his offering he did not look with favor. So Cain was very angry, and his face was downcast." ⁶ Then the Lord said to Cain, "Why are you angry? Why is your face downcast? ⁷ If you do what is right, will you not be accepted? But if you do not do what is right, sin is crouching at your door; it desires to have you, but you must rule over it. (NIV).*

Here we see that Cain brought "some." His brother brought the firstborn. Or in other words, his first fruits. Abel gave his first and best while Cain just brought something. God's reply explains how He sees Cain's offering. Basically, telling him you know what you brought wasn't right. He also explained that not giving his best with his whole heart will affect his emotions and his actions.

In today's vernacular we would say that Cain was tight with his money. A scrooge. We have all met people like this. They come across cheap and selfish. They aren't happy people. They tend to be grumpy and angry. They're the kind of person when asked to chip in for something or someone they respond with their usual excuse or a "why should I?" They'd easily ask you to pay but never return the favor. In plain English, they're greedy.

This is why Jesus said in Matthew 6:24 *"No man can serve two masters: for either he will hate the one, and love the other; or else he will hold to the one, and despise the other. Ye cannot serve God and mammon."* (KJV). The word mammon means wealth or material things. Jesus explains why God requires tithe. You can't love both. Like Cain, you will love one and hate the other. He hated enough to kill his brother Abel. Tithing is one of the easiest ways to know if you have made Jesus Lord of your life or simply tried to add Him to it but under your terms.

It's a principle of His kingdom. We give because He first gave. It teaches us His heart for us and others. Luke 6:38 says, *"Give, and it will be given to you: good measure, pressed down, shaken together, and running over will be put* into your bosom. For with the same measure that you use, it will be measured back to you" (NKJV).

Principle 2: "Bring the whole tithe into the storehouse, that there may be food in My house."

Your tithe is to be given to the local church you attend. The storehouse was located at the tabernacle. In today's language, it would be the church you attend. This not only served to care for those who gave their lives for the service of the tabernacle, but God also commanded a blessing regarding obedience to this. Deuteronomy 28:8 says, "The LORD shall command the blessing upon thee in thy storehouses, and in all that thou settest thine hand unto; and he shall bless thee in the land which the LORD thy God giveth thee" (KJV). God commands a special blessing on the work of your hands for caring for the church and its shepherds.

I find it no coincidence that God provided for me from within the church. It's a beautiful example of why we give our tithes. There was "food" in His house to meet my need. This very example is why God requires the tithe. When God prepared Moses to take the children of Israel into their promised land, he gave each tribe a piece of land for their inheritance. All received except the tribe of Levi. The Lord told them that He himself was their inheritance. Their needs were to be met from the Lord's portion. Since they give their lives to His service,

He is the one who meets their needs. What is the Lord's portion? It is the tenth. He would use the tithe that belonged to him to care for them. This tithing practice assured that both those who minister and those who had needs could have their needs met by the Lord.

Isn't that beautiful? He planned beforehand and was thinking about us first. He prepared to meet our needs before we asked. His character is so eloquently on display. God had prepared a garden before He created man so that man would have a place ready for him where all his needs would be met. That's the God we serve! Before you knew you needed a savior, He had a plan, and His name was Jesus. He came and died to pay the debt you could never pay. That's our God. He's the same yesterday, today, and forever. You can count on Him!

Principle 3: *"Test me in this," says the Lord Almighty.*

This is the one place in scripture that actually tells us to test Him. He wants to prove to you, as He did to me that Sunday night, *"My God shall supply all your needs according to His riches in glory by Christ Jesus"* Philippians 4:19 (NKJV).

God is no respecter of persons. What He does for one, He will do for the other. He's a good father. He longs to give good gifts to His children. He wants to do for you as He did for me. He is watching you as He did me that day. He has blessings stored up in His store-

YOU DON'T NEED MONEY, YOU JUST NEED GOD

house. He beckons us to try Him. *Taste and see that the Lord is good* (Psalms 34:8 NIV). His promise to this test says, *"Test me in this," says the Lord Almighty, "and see if I will not throw open the floodgates of heaven and pour out so much blessing that there will not be room enough to store it. ¹¹ I will prevent pests from devouring your crops, and the vines in your fields will not drop their fruit before it is ripe," says the Lord Almighty* (NIV).

What an amazing promise. This covenant means that if we give to God His portion, He will protect all that I have. He promises to provide more than we can even receive. He wants to bless you.

If you have not brought your finances into covenant with God, then I want to challenge you today to try Him. Test Him and see for yourself. If you feel like you have disobeyed God in this or allowed money and material things to have your affections, then simply repent. God will forgive you and wipe your slate clean. You can join hands with Jesus and start fresh today.

Now look at the needs you face today and declare out loud with all your heart...

You don't need money. You just need God.

PRAYER

Lord, you know my need even before I call on you. You know my frame and that I am only dust. Lead me according to your word and your promises. Strengthen me to trust you more. Guide me into all of your truth and may I find my security not in the world's idea of it, but only in you. In Jesus's name, Amen.

CHAPTER 4

What's the Formula?

Judy Mercer

I can still see the look of utter discouragement and panic on my mother's face. That was a look that I had never seen before. It was riveting to me. You have to know my mother to grasp my concern. Being divorced and a single parent was not the norm back in the day. Dad's alcoholic binges would bring him in and out of our lives, causing stress, turmoil, and conflict. Life was difficult and finances weren't just tight, they were a juggernaut.

Mom worked very hard to hold it all together. To her, it didn't matter that she didn't have anyone to lean on for help. She leaned wholly on the Lord. Her lack and loneliness forged a deep well of faith and prayer in her life. No matter the need, she turned to God in prayer. No matter what rose up against her, she stood her ground in God and on His promises! She was a real prayer warrior and had no fear of the future or the devil! It was this tenacious and warrior-like faith that made God so real to us, and we saw first-hand that our God is an ever-present help!

Seeing that look on my mother's face that day was shocking. We were raised to never give in to fear and never back down from the devil. So, what could possibly have happened to my mom that she looked so defeated?

She made up her mind that our kitchen needed new flooring. Not being one to rely on anyone, all the while keeping the cost at the barest minimum, she took it upon herself to tackle the job. She bought the linoleum tiles, and the big black can of tar to seal them down. We had a fairly long kitchen that flowed into a good-sized 'nook,' as well as the laundry room. She worked all day long, all by herself, laying tile after tile until late into the night.

Being thoroughly exhausted she had decided to wait until the next morning to clean all the tar from around the set tiles and finish it up. To her utter shock and dismay, when she started to clean the tiles the next morning, that tar wouldn't budge! She desperately tried everything she could lay her hands on to get that tar up. Absolutely nothing worked. All that back-breaking work. And the kitchen floor looked worse than it had before.

Of course, mom prayed. Then it came to her. She remembered the testimony she had heard about a missionary in another country. He had planted a grove of trees and a severe devastating frost had hit the entire region. Everyone around him were losing their groves and crops, one after the other. In his desperation he prayed and asked the Lord what he should do? How could he save his groves? In that time of prayer God gave him a 'formula' that he was instructed to place in fire pots and set throughout his grove of trees. By faith he made that formula, put it in the pots and set them throughout his groves just as God told him. Can you believe it? He didn't lose one tree. Our all-wise, all-knowing God who created this earth and all that's in it, had revealed to that faithful missionary what to do in his hour of crisis.

As that missionary's testimony rose up in my mother's mind and heart, she thought to herself, "Well God, if you can do that for that missionary, by giving him the formula that he needed, you can show ME how to get this tar up off this floor!" So, she prayed, and looked to God for the answer in her hour of crisis as well.

She was working at that time as a bookkeeper for a local business. The owner's wife had become friends with my mom, and she just happened to stop by the office just a few days later. Mom was sharing with her the lament of her tile story. The woman said, "Alice, I think I know something that can take up that tar. It contains ether. You will have to work fast. Keep all the windows open, but I think it might do the trick for you." Well, my mom was 'game on!' She got that product and cleaned up that tile floor lickety-split!

Once again, we learned money isn't always the answer. Sometimes you need God's wisdom and guidance. Sometimes you need God-appointed connections. Sometimes you need answers and solutions that you can only find through prayer. It's been said that crisis will show you what you rely on!

PLAY CALL: Know that *God is lord over every crisis – big or little!*

I learned from that tile floor lesson that God is able to help you with everything and in every area of your life. There is no dilemma or disappointment that can't be figured out or overturned by turning to God. He will be the ultimate resource for *all* of your life. You may feel you have 'botched the job' or have made things worse and you just don't know how to fix it! But Jeremiah 33:3 says, *"Call to me and I will answer you, and will tell you great and hidden things that you have not known"* (ESV). God is the answer for every crisis or confusion you will ever face. My mom's kitchen tile floor is the perfect example of this truth.

GOD IS LORD OVER EVERY CRISIS
What's the Formula?

Principle 1: *God is relational.*

Once in prayer, I was sort of 'complaining' to the Lord. I was asking Him, "Lord, why do I have to pray over and over for answers to come? Why can't I just ask You once and have you answer right away? Didn't you say ask and you shall receive?" Immediately up out of my spirit came this response: *"If I answered you immediately when you first asked, you would then rise up and go on your way and not be seeking Me. Isn't the whole reason I chose you and saved you was for us to have a relationship together? Did I save your lost soul just to give you answers to your prayers or did I choose you to know Me, to have intimate fellowship with Me, to commune with Me, and be one in spirit with Me?"* Ouch! That certainly changed my mind set about prayer.

Of course, He will answer when we pray, but we also should desire that our relationship with the Lord is our *first* desire. We are called the Bride of Christ. That means we are to do life together. And in doing life together, He will guide us through every obstacle, provide wisdom and counsel for every crisis, and see to it that we are in the right place, at the right time because of our relationship with Him. Jeremiah 29:13 – *"You will seek me and find me, when you seek me with all your heart"* (NIV).

You were created by a loving, relational God who designed you to be in a loving relationship with Him. The purpose of God creating Adam and Eve was for fellowship and friendship. We read how Enoch walked with God. Abraham was called the friend of God. Throughout the Old Testament and New Testament, we read "I have called you by name."

Jesus said, "My sheep know My voice."

Jesus's prayer for us in John 17:3 was *"And this is eternal life, that they know you the only true God, and Jesus Christ whom You have sent"* (ESV). Everything we receive from the Lord flows out of our personal relationship with Him. This is where it all begins. Knowing that we were created to know Him personally, we can then easily turn to Him and share everything in our lives with Him. James 4:8 tells us to *"come close to God and He will come close to you"* (NLT).

Principle 2: *It requires time in prayer.*

Prayer is the ultimate act of a relationship with God. Jeremiah 29:12-13 - *"Then you will call upon Me and come and pray to Me, and I will hear you. You will seek Me and find Me, when you seek Me with all your heart"* (NIV). It was my mother's consistent pattern of prayer in her life that enabled her to find the answers she needed at all times, for every situation. We often relegate prayer to a 9-1-1 call or what we do only in a crisis or time of desperation.

I have learned from my mother's example that being faithful in prayer, faithful to my relationship with God, He in turn is faithful to me in every part of my life.

Each and every time the Patriarchs went to a new place, they always built an altar first and called upon the name of the Lord! They made sure to first have a place to pray! Jesus told His disciple in John 15:7 *"If you abide in me, and my words abide in you, ask whatever you wish, and it will be done for you"* (ESV).

Principle 3: *Remember answered prayers!*

It was my mother's 'remembering' the missionary's miracle that spurred her faith in God. By remembering the past miracle, she was able to lay hold of a present miracle. Over and over in God's Word we are admonished 'to remember.'

Israel was instructed to 'build memorials' for the many miracles God performed on their behalf. Joshua 4:6 *"We will use these stones to build a memorial. In the future your children will ask you, 'What do these stones mean?'"* (NLT). It was the rehearsing of how God had helped them before that would produce a faith for what He would do in their lives now. We need to hear the testimonies from others to build up our faith.

We need to be remembering all the times that God has already answered us and helped us. The miracles and faithfulness He has provided in our lives and in the lives of others will encourage us to release our faith for what God will do right now. Matthew 19:26 *"But Jesus looked at them and said, 'With man this is impossible, but with God all things are possible'"* (ESV).

There is no need that you have, that God can't do something about it today. Seek the one who knows it all. Ask the one who owns it all. Trust in the one who provides it all. And remember, you don't need money. You just need God.

PRAYER

Lord, I'm grateful for the privilege of knowing you and you offering me a relationship with you. Help me to remember that I can ask you for wisdom no matter if my need is great or small. I give you permission to remind me to stop and ask you first since you delight in knowing me and helping me. You are the answer to every question, and you desire to share the answers with me. I thank you for all these things. In Jesus's name, Amen.

CHAPTER 5

Hidden Provision

Jaime Luce

The room was romantically lit by the natural sunset that came streaming through the endless wall of windows, illuminating the waves crashing onto the rocks below. The room was filled with tropical floral arrangements large and small. The greenery was so lush it could have been outside. Elegant music filled the air inviting us in as the hostess led us to the table that had been prepared for us.

When we'd finished our dinner, our waiter came to offer us dessert. He stepped toward me as he opened a beautiful gold dome serving container to show me the feature that evening. As he opened the lid, Joel slid out of his chair and onto one knee as the diamond ring was revealed sitting on top of a bed of flower pedals. "Will you marry me?"

Time stood still. I could tell that everyone in the restaurant was watching us. It was as if they were all holding their breath with Joel, waiting for my reply. And with a very enthusiastic "YES! Yes, I'll marry you" the silence was broken and the whole restaurant erupted in applause.

We were getting married. That's the good news. The bad news was I only had two months to plan the wedding. But the first order of business was to find a place to live. This was the tricky part. With a seven-year-old little boy and a five-year-old little girl, we needed a house with three bedrooms, and we had hoped for a yard. We knew that most people start off with an apartment, but after praying and asking the Lord what direction we should go, we knew in our hearts that we needed a home. We knew that the Lord wanted us to have a home.

We had worked out our budget. And like most new couples, it was going to be tight. Our top dollar was $1,500 a month. We eagerly began the search. Sadly, it didn't take long for total disappointment to sink in. We found only one home for rent in the town we felt God directed us to live in. They wanted $1,700 and they wouldn't budge. It couldn't be done. We just couldn't afford that.

We were running out of time. The wedding was a little less than a month away, and we didn't have a place to live. This was supposed to be a beautiful new beginning for both of us. We knew that God had brought us together and that He had a plan for us. We knew the city we were to live in. This wasn't making sense. How could there be no available homes? And with no additional money, even if another house became available, we could not afford more than $1,500 a month.

We had just seen God provide Joel with a new job. God was our source. We continued to encourage one another. If He did it once, He would do it again. We knew no matter what it looked like, *We didn't need money. We just needed God.* He had a place for us, and He would provide. We held on, trusting that the Lord would make a way for us.

On a Saturday afternoon we decided to drive around town and just look one more time. As we drove past the storefronts, I noticed a realtor's office. I felt the Holy Spirit nudge me. We needed to stop and go inside. As we opened the door, a tall senior gentleman with white hair welcomed us in. We told him what we were looking for and what price we could afford. He thought for a moment and told us he only knew of one property. It was the one that we'd already seen. He said he wanted to look through his files.

There was a tall dark brown four drawer file cabinet against the paneled wall. As he walked over to it, something caught his eye. He leaned over and saw a piece of paper caught between the wall and the cabinet. He reached behind it to pick it up. He said he didn't know about this house and wondered how long this listing had been there. It was a rental listing. If they didn't know about it, no one did since they were the only listing agent with this rental listing. Our hearts leapt. Could this be our house?

He began reading all the specs and said he could show it to us if we were interested. As much as I loved what I was hearing, the big question was how much was it? It wouldn't matter how perfect it was if it was over our budget. I blurted out, "How much is it?" He told us $1,500 a month. I squealed. "Can we look at it now?" He said, "yes" and we went right over.

God had hidden it. He knew what we needed and when we'd need it, and He wasn't going to let someone else have it. It was not only adorable, but was in a gated community, the very size we needed, and exactly the price we could afford. It had three bedrooms and a park-like back yard complete with bunnies, squirrels, and fruit trees. God cared not just that we had a house but that we had our hearts' desire. This was the beginning of our life of faith and finance as a married couple. The Lord was declaring to us again that *you don't need money. You just need God.*

PLAY CALL: *Trust and Obey.*

There is an old hymn written by John Henry Sammis titled "Trust and Obey." The lyrics say, "Trust and obey, for there's no other way to be happy in Jesus, but to trust and obey." When you know that you have heard the Lord's promise or instruction, don't harden your heart because of doubt. Lay hold of it by faith and keep believing. Trust what you heard from the Lord and obey his instructions and leadings. He knows what He has for you and exactly where it is. If we had not stopped in that realtor's office, we would never have known about our house. He led us to what He had hidden for us. If you will ask Him, He will lead you as well. Trust and obey Him. There really isn't another way.

TRUST AND OBEY
Hidden Provision

Sometimes the financial need is not simply for more money. Sometimes what we already have, is all we need. Joel and I had a budget. We also had a specific need for a home. What we needed wasn't more money. We needed the right home within the budget we could afford. We weren't asking for more than we what we needed. However, what we needed wasn't visible to us. It was hidden. The beautiful part is that it wasn't hidden from us but instead it was hidden *for* us. There's a big difference.

The scripture tells us in Proverbs 25:2 that *"It is the glory of God to conceal a thing: but the honor of kings is to search out a matter"* (KJV). I'm convinced that had we not sought God for the answer, it would have remained hidden from us. However, we sought the Lord. In seeking

Him we had the honor of finding what He had hidden for us. It was in the seeking that we looked with expectation. It was by the prompting of the Holy Spirit, and the following of his instructions, that we stopped into the realtor's office that day. It is God's pleasure to share His hidden treasures with you. It's like a game of hide and seek with His children, or an egg hunt. You search and find the eggs He's filled with candy. He enjoys seeing you find it and enjoy what He's prepared.

The Lord wants you to know the answer. You will find example after example in the Bible of those who asked the Lord for help, and how they received it. My mother says, "It's not that the Bible says so much. It just says the same thing over and over again." Looking for the answer isn't difficult. Looking is what brings you the honor as well as the answer.

Mark's 6:34-43 account of Jesus feeding the five thousand gives us a blueprint. Most of the miracles you will receive will come by this same blueprint:

> [34] *When Jesus landed and saw a large crowd, he had compassion on them, because they were like sheep without a shepherd. So he began teaching them many things.* [35] *By this time it was late in the day, so his disciples came to him. "This is a remote place,"* *they said, "and it's already very late.* [36] *Send the people away so that they can go to the surrounding*

countryside and villages and buy themselves some-thing to eat." ³⁷ But he answered, "You give them something to eat." They said to him, "That would take more than half a year's wages! Are we to go and spend that much on bread and give it to them to eat?" ³⁸ "How many loaves do you have?" he asked. "Go and see." When they found out, they said, "Five—and two fish." ³⁹ Then Jesus directed them to have all the people sit down in groups on the green grass. ⁴⁰ So they sat down in groups of hundreds and fifties. ⁴¹ Taking the five loaves and the two fish and looking up to heaven, he gave thanks and broke the loaves. Then he gave them to his disciples to dis-tribute to the people. He also divided the two fish among them all. ⁴² They all ate and were satisfied, ⁴³and the disciples picked up twelve basketfuls of broken pieces of bread and fish. (NIV)

The text lays out three principles we can learn from and put into practice for our own needs. It really isn't difficult. God's ways are not tedious. The Bible is a pic-ture book of sorts. The illustrations are great teachers if we are willing to learn and apply their wisdom.

Principle 1: *Bring the problem to Jesus.*

Trust that He is your answer. In verses 35-36, the dis-ciples tell Jesus the problem. ³⁵ *By this time it was late in the day, so his disciples came to him. "This is a remote place," they said, "and it's already very late. ³⁶ Send the people away so that they can go to the surrounding countryside and villages and buy themselves something to eat"* (NIV).

What they expected was for Jesus to make the problem go away. Admittedly this is what we always want but rarely does this happen. As children of God, we don't ever have to be afraid of the problems we face. We may not know the answer but when you have Jesus, you have the answer.

Jesus does something unexpected here. He tells the disciples to handle it. ³⁷ *But he answered, "You give them something to eat"* (NIV). Have you ever felt like God was playing hot potato with you? You get it passed off to Jesus and feel so relieved but then He tosses it back into your lap. "But don't you get it Jesus? I don't know what to do. How do you expect me to handle this?"

It reminds me of the passage in 2 Kings 4:1-7:

> ¹*A certain woman of the wives of the sons of the prophets cried out to Elisha, saying, "Your servant my husband is dead, and you know that your servant feared the Lord. And the creditor is coming to take my two sons to be his slaves." ² So Elisha said to her, "What shall I do for you? Tell me, what do you have in the house?" And she said, "Your maidservant has nothing in the house but a jar of oil." ³ Then*

he said, "Go, borrow vessels from everywhere, from all your neighbors—empty vessels; do not gather just a few. ⁴And when you have come in, you shall shut the door behind you and your sons; then pour it into all those vessels, and set aside the full ones." ⁵So she went from him and shut the door behind her and her sons, who brought the vessels to her; and she poured it out. ⁶ Now it came to pass, when the vessels were full, that she said to her son, "Bring me another vessel." And he said to her, "There is not another vessel." So the oil ceased. ⁷Then she came and told the man of God. And he said, "Go, sell the oil and pay your debt; and you and your sons live on the rest." (NKJV)

Elisha tells this poor widow, in the anguish of her mess, "What shall I do for you?" Then he puts it back on her. "Tell me, what do you have in the house?" And she said, "Your maidservant has nothing in the house but a jar of oil." Here Elisha asks her "what do you have?" This exchange was exactly what Jesus did in Mark's gospel. Jesus asked his disciples, ³⁸ "How many loaves do you have?" he asked. "Go and see." When they found out, they said, "Five—and two fish."

Joel and I brought our need to the Lord. He essentially asked us, "What do you have?" And we told Him we have $1,500. God may be asking you. So, what is it that you have? Whatever you have is exactly what you need. This also happened in Exodus 4:1-5:

> ¹*Then Moses answered and said, "But suppose they will not believe me or listen to my voice; suppose they say, 'The Lord has not appeared to you.'"* ² *So the Lord said to him, "What is that in your hand?" He said, "A rod." * ³ *And He said, "Cast it on the ground." So, he cast it on the ground, and it became a serpent; and Moses fled from it. * ⁴ *Then the Lord said to Moses, "Reach out your hand and take it by the tail" (and he reached out his hand and caught it, and it became a rod in his hand), * ⁵ *"that they may believe that the Lord God of their fathers, the God of Abraham, the God of Isaac, and the God of Jacob, has appeared to you." (NKJV)*

Here we see God challenging Moses with the same question. What do you have in your hand? You may only have a little oil like the widow. You may have only a couple of fish and some bread like the disciples. You may have a stick like Moses. It may seem insignificant. It may seem worthless. But in God's hands, it's all you need.

Principle 2. *Follow His instructions.*

In other words. OBEY. ³⁹*"Then Jesus directed them to have all the people sit down in groups on the green grass. * ⁴⁰ *So* *they sat down in groups of hundreds and fifties*" (NIV). This seems to be where people have an issue. So many times, the instructions we hear from the Lord don't make sense to our natural minds.

We seem to forget that God is the creator. His ways and thoughts are higher than ours. Isaiah 55:8-9 *⁸"For My thoughts are not your thoughts, Nor are your ways My ways," says the Lord. ⁹ "For as the heavens are higher than the earth, So, are My ways higher than your ways, And My thoughts than your thoughts"* (NKJV).

It didn't make sense to stop into the realtor's office that day. We had already been given a list of what was available. We had even looked through every real-estate magazine in the area. But the Holy Spirit is never wrong. Remember how it is the honor of kings to search out a matter? The scripture tells us in 1 Corinthians 2:10 *"But God has revealed them to us through His Spirit. For the Spirit searches all things, yes, the deep things of God"* (NKJV).

Relying on the Holy Spirit instead of your own, will lead you into the deep and hidden things God has for you. They are not naturally perceived. They are spiritually discerned. If you don't have the Holy Spirit, you can ask for Him. Bring that need to Jesus. If all you have is an open heart, that is all you need. According to Luke 11:13, the Holy Spirit is a gift from God: *"If you then, being evil, know how to give good gifts to your children, how much more will your heavenly Father give the Holy Spirit to those who ask Him!"* (NKJV). Having the Holy Spirit gives us access to hidden information.

Without a word of instruction, we are left to our own deducing powers in any given situation. Though God was good to us and gave us all a brain to think with and a free will to choose with, why intentionally make decisions blindly and without His guidance, simply hoping for the best? You could instead follow instructions that lead to a sure and intended end.

The outcomes for both the widow with Elijah and Moses would have been entirely different had they relied on their own ideas and thoughts instead of listening to the instructions they were given. For the widow, she'd have had a loss of her sons to pay a debt with no future means to live on. Instead, her debt was paid and she and her sons were free and prosperous. For Moses, his family, and an entire nation, slavery and death would have continued. Instead, freedom and prosperity were won for all. Coming to God is the first step but listening to and following His instructions is paramount.

We read in Proverbs 3:5-6 *"Trust in the Lord with all your heart and lean not on your own understanding; In all your ways acknowledge Him, and He shall direct your paths"* (NKJV). A quick google search will tell you that in any given day a person will make approximately 30,000 conscious decisions. It seems abundantly clear that we do use the minds we were given. What amazes me, is that so many people who consider themselves Christians, rarely ask the Lord for direction and guidance in their day to day lives when so many things need to be decided.

This scripture says to acknowledge the Lord in *ALL* your ways. Think about that for a minute. How often do you acknowledge Him in your decisions? Is it only on rare occasions when you think you don't know what to do? Is it when you're in trouble? Is it only with really big decisions? Or do you ever?

He actually waits with longing for us to seek Him. His desire is to have a real and tangible relationship where you discuss all that's on your heart and where you listen to what is on His. The reason for this is not to restrain you but to bless you. He knows what you can't know. He sees what you can't see. His heart is to lead and guide you into the plan and blessing He has waiting to give you. Asking God for His guidance could actually make the difference in a bad or good decision. His leading could help you discover God's hidden blessings.

Joel and I knew we could make a decision on where to live. It was not that we might make a wrong decision. We didn't even hope for a good decision. We wanted God's best. We knew what our parameters were, but we also knew that God is not limited by our parameters. He can do exceedingly and abundantly more than we could ask or think, according to Ephesians 3:20. Asking Him for His help and leading would open up doors we could not open on our own. In our case, He had a hidden door waiting for us. A blessing reserved just for us.

Matthew 7:7 says, *"Ask and it will be given to you; seek and you will find; knock and the door will be opened to you"* (NIV).

Principle 3: *Thank the Lord for His provision even before you see it.*

[41] *"Taking the five loaves and the two fish and looking up to heaven, he gave thanks and broke the loaves. Then he gave them to his disciples to distribute to the people. He also divided the two fish among them all.* [42] *They all ate and were satisfied, 43 and the disciples picked up twelve basketfuls of broken pieces of bread and fish"* (NIV).

Jesus had not broken the bread yet when He thanked the Father, and neither should you. Thank Him first. Thank Him that you can come to Him with any and all needs. Thank Him that He has assured you that what you have is enough, in His hands. Thank Him that He sees you and has compassion on you. Thank Him that He isn't limited to what you can see. Thank Him because He's good. For every reason you can, thank Him. He's a good Father.

When God meets the need there is always plenty to spare. You will be satisfied. You won't be left wanting. Psalms 23:1 says, *"The Lord is my shepherd; I shall not want"*

(NKJV). This is His promise to you. You may feel that at the present your provision is hidden. You don't see it, and you don't see how. Don't worry. Take your need to the Father. Listen for His instructions. And thank Him, for the answer is on its way.

Now look at the needs you face today and declare out loud with all your heart...*You don't need money. You just need God.*

PRAYER

Lord you said in Your word that there is nothing hidden that You won't uncover. Would You uncover the answer to my need? Show me where to look and guide me with Your eye. Open a door that no man can close. And close the door You don't want me to walk through, letting no man open it. Keep me in the safe place of Your blessing. And now I thank You because I know that You have heard me, and You will answer. In Jesus's name, Amen.

CHAPTER 6

When God is Your Realtor

Judy Mercer

There was a daily gnawing restlessness inside of me. An uncomfortableness that relentlessly poked at my mind and heart. We simply needed more room. We needed a bigger house. We had to have more space. I realized I had to face that fact, and I knew what I then needed to do. Seek the will and mind of God in prayer. But this prayer time would astound and challenge me in ways I could never have imagined. I was completely rocked to say the least.

"Surely that could NOT be the answer to my prayer! – God could NOT be saying what I was hearing." I have to be getting this wrong. Did the Lord actually tell me to sell my house by owner? That had to be the most ridiculous idea to ever come into my head. I immediately stopped praying. I had to digest this whole ludicrous notion. How could God ever expect me to do such an absurd undertaking? But I knew there was no mistaking what I had heard in my spirit. This answer wasn't coming from my mind. And I knew it. This was nothing that I would have ever considered. But deep within my heart, I knew the Holy Spirit was speaking directly to me. It was as if someone were sitting right beside me and simply talking to me, and I could not mistake what was being said.

My husband Jim and I had been feeling for months that we needed to buy a bigger home. Our kids were becoming teenagers and the bathrooms were in short supply. We knew we needed to quit talking about it and make it happen. Yet the glitch was we didn't want to move to any other part of town. We wanted our kids in their same schools and we loved the surrounding lush green hills and ambiance where we were. This limited us to a very restricted portion of real estate.

It was a packed, full time in our lives. Both Jim and I were working. Jim was also traveling throughout the western states in the Californian's Gospel Quartet, including venues at Disneyland, Knott's Berry Farm, and the Queen Mary. They were making recordings in the studio as well as having a heavy practice schedule. As always, we were in key areas of leadership responsibilities at church. To top it off, it was Easter time. I had undertaken to write and direct an Easter drama/musical presentation and Jim was directing the choir. By all accounts, this was not the time to be buying and selling a house.

Hearing those words, 'sell your house by owner,' I wailed before God. "How could I ever do that Lord? I'm no real estate agent, and I know nothing about the legalities involved." I offered up protest after protest. I really thought God didn't understand that this was beyond my capabilities. Finally, when I had exhausted every legitimate reason I could come up with, again, that still small voice began to speak to my heart. I began hearing things like, just get out your paperwork on your current house, use that as a model, and make the necessary changes to fit your new situation. The escrow company will handle all the legal aspects that you'll need. Wow, what a thought! And now I would have to tell Jim about this crazy notion.

Going to work that next week, where I worked as an executive assistant to the president of a publishing company, one of the directors came into our office. They stated they needed to publish an ad that will run in their full circulation for a test they were doing. They wanted to see which areas draw the most response. I had intended to run a small ad, but it would only have been in my surrounding area. This test run would cover the entire southern California basin. I spoke up and said that I have an ad to sell our house. They lit up like a Christmas tree and said a real estate ad would be perfect! Could we please use your ad to run for our test? There it was again! You don't need money. You just need God.

Within the first few days of that ad placement, we received a call from a gentleman completely out of our area. As a single parent, he was looking for a nice community in which to raise his two sons. He made an appointment with us to see the house. He was a cash buyer at our full asking price – no negotiations required! What could be any easier? I could hardly believe what the Lord had done. I would never have placed an ad where that man lived. Yet the Lord had orchestrated the means to get our ad to the very man who would purchase our home.

We had stipulated in the paperwork that we would only sell our home on the condition that we found another home – that the escrows would close concurrently. He was fine with that – at first. Our slammed schedules at this Easter time left us no room to even look for a new house. And our options were so limited because we would only move within a few miles' radius. I was feeling the pressure. Having constant Easter production rehearsals, working full time, Jim's travel schedule and fielding this man's phone calls about what progress we were making to consummate the deal, was getting heavy. We had always trusted that if we take care of God's house, He will take care of our house. And God has always honored that commitment. We have passed that same conviction on to our children as well. One particular Saturday, when waking up that early morning, I had a deep foreboding inside me. I just knew that this man was not going to wait any longer! I felt nervous and worried. It had been weeks now and his phone calls were becoming more pressing...he wanted a home for his boys.

We had been seriously searching yet could find nothing. At that moment while contemplating the seriousness of the crossroads we were facing, something inside me felt wrong. I recognized that I just had no joy over the sale of our house. It didn't feel like a victory even though we had a cash buyer at our full asking price. Something had to be wrong. I knew I should be doing a happy dance at what the Lord had done.

I went to the Lord in prayer. "Lord", I prayed, "I don't understand why I don't have any shout of victory in my heart. You have been so good to help us every step of the way. Please speak to me Lord. Help me to understand." In that moment it came into my spirit – "you're not asking enough money for this house." "Oh no!" I said to the Lord, "but we can't go back on the deal. We already agreed to that asking price." But the inner instruction just wouldn't budge. "You're not asking enough for this house." I knew we had to obey God, and we couldn't go through with the sale at that price. I resigned myself to the idea that this would certainly kill the deal.

The next time the gentleman called, I had to bravely tell him that with what is on the market, we just weren't asking enough money for the house. The phone went silent. My heart dropped to my feet. And then I heard him say, "Well, how much then do you want?" Slowly I gave him the new figure the Lord had spoken to me and after a long pause, He answered, "I can do that." Oh, my goodness. NOW I felt joy! NOW I felt the victory! NOW I did the happy dance at the goodness of God. I learned such an important lesson through that. I learned to wait on the "witness" of the Holy Spirit. When God is doing something on your behalf, your spirit will be rejoicing. You will absolutely know you have the victory.

And in the words of Paul Harvey, the late radio broadcaster, "and now, for the rest of the story." With the new price point settled, I promptly called my sister who had just bought a new house herself and asked for the name of her realtor. He called back almost immediately and already had several houses for us to look at. Jim and I quickly jumped in the car and off we went. In what felt like a New York minute, we found our dream home that very day! Located only one mile from our current location, it had just come on the market that very morning.

It was a robust seller's market at the time and the house already had several offers submitted. Now we needed to seek the Lord for the price He wanted us to pay. Believing in Proverbs 3:6 NLT, "*Seek His will in all you do, and He will show you which path to take"* (NIV), we prayed together.

Jim and I have learned that when it is God's will for us, we both will be in agreement. If we don't agree, then we don't do anything. We keep praying until there is agreement. After asking each other, "what do you hear God saying?" – we both had heard the exact same number. It was less than the asking price and we knew other offers were being made. Yet, we also knew you have to do God's will, God's way. So, we called the realtor and gave him our counteroffer.

The next day he called us back with great excitement in his voice. Our counteroffer was just $2,000 below their final price. The deal could be sealed within the hour. Now we understood that $2,000 over a 30-year loan wouldn't really matter. It seemed like a no-brainer. But that was not the number God had spoken to us. We knew immediately that we could pay that $2,000 easily, but I also knew that the mortgage was then forever on us. Yet if we obeyed God and paid what He had told us, the mortgage would be on God, and He would always take care of it. Yet how do we explain that to someone who is not a believer? Jim called our realtor back and calmly said 'we are sorry, but we have to hold to the offer we made." There was dead silence on the phone. He politely thanked us and hung up.

I cried. I loved that house. Jim loved that house. But now it was gone. As we sat digesting the ramifications of what had occurred, the phone rang again. This time I answered it and heard our realtor's voice saying, "I know that's your house. I just know it. I'm going to give you the $2,000 difference." I was shocked. I was worried. Were we being tricked somehow to not pay what God had said to us? In my confusion I thought I wasn't understanding this right. I asked him if we could call him back. He was stunned of course, and slowly replied, "Okay." I turned to Jim and told him what he had said about giving us the $2,000. "Jim, is this a trick?" I asked. He just laughed at me and said, "Honey, this is God." And it was! He called him right back and greatly thanked him and said we would be thrilled to accept his kind offer. We had our dream home, and we also knew we had God's blessing.

We quickly called the buyer of our current home and told him the good news. I don't know who was happier, us or our buyer. Both homes were consummated, and we moved within weeks. God proved to be the best real estate agent we could have ever asked for. We're told the best scenario in real estate is "sell high, buy low." And that is exactly the way it happened. That house was a constant source of blessing for the next fifteen years. It still lingers in our memories of all the good things that happened to our family while living where God had chosen for us.

PLAY CALL: *The blessing is in the obedience.*

Everything with the Lord is bound up in our willingness to obey Him. We so often make our prayers and petitions to Him. Yet there remains that fundamental issue of obeying what He speaks to us or directs us to do. Jesus's words could not be more clear. "Follow Me." We are not to do the leading but the following. Over and over in the Bible are the accounts of miracles that God did when people obeyed what He told them to do. *"Then Jesus said to His disciples, "If anyone desires to come after Me, let him deny himself, and take us his cross, and follow Me,"* Matthew 16:24 (NKJV). It has been said the cross we take up is when our will crosses God's will. Will we surrender to God's will and obey whatever He would ask us to do? I really didn't want to sell my house by owner... I really didn't want to tell our cash buyer that now we needed more money... I really didn't want to risk losing the new house we had just found over a mere $2,000 – but I also knew God's basic principle from 1 Samuel 15:22-23 *"And Samuel said, Has the Lord as great delight in burnt offerings and sacrifices, as in obeying the voice of the Lord? Behold, to obey is better than sacrifice and to listen than the fat of rams. For rebellion is as the sin of divination, and presumption is as iniquity and idolatry...."* (ESV). God spoke through the prophet Isaiah to His people saying, *"If you are willing and obedient, you shall eat the good of the land; but if you refuse and rebel, you shall be eaten by the sword; for the mouth of the Lord has spoken"* (Isaiah 1:19-20, ESV). The importance of our obedience is bound up in our willingness. This scripture clearly reveals that before we can obey, our hearts must first be willing. When I have trouble obeying the Lord, I begin to ask the Holy Spirit, who is our Helper, to help me be willing. It is in the surrendering of our will to God's will and then walking out in surrender through obedience to His voice and His direction that the answers come.

THE BLESSING IS IN THE OBEDIENCE
When God is Your Realtor

Principle 1: *Foster the time and relationship to know the voice of the Lord.*

First and foremost, it is about our personal relationship with Jesus. Jesus said in John 10:27, *"My sheep hear My voice, and I know them, and they follow Me"* (NKJV). This makes it so clear. When you really know someone, you learn their voice. And the more you know someone, the more quickly you recognize their voice. Just as that is true in the natural, it is also true in the spiritual. *"God is spirit, and those who worship Him must worship in spirit and truth"* (NKJV). John 3:6. It is spirit-to-spirit communication. Psalms 85:8 says, *"I listen carefully to what God the LORD is saying, for He speaks peace to His faithful people. But let them not return to their foolish ways"* (NLT). It is time spent with the Lord, in prayer and in His Word, where we learn to know Him and what His voice sounds like. We learn the way He speaks to us. The more time we give to Him, the more easily we hear from Him. The more time we invest in having a personal relationship with Jesus, the more He speaks into our lives and directs our steps. It was because of our relationship with the Lord and hearing God's voice that enabled His miracle power to manifest in our lives in such a practical and victorious way. John 17:3 sums it up in saying, *"And this is eternal life, that they know You, the only true God, and Jesus Christ whom You have sent"* (ESV). That is our privilege as born-again Believers. We can know Him and He does speak when we are willing and obedient. 1 John 2:3 *"And by this we know that we have come to know Him, if we keep His commandments"* (ESV). Learning the voice of your shepherd will benefit you in every area of your life.

Principle 2: *Be sensitive to the witness of the Holy Spirit.*

As the Good Shepherd spoken of in Psalms 23, He leads us into green pastures and beside still waters. I have come to recognize those "still waters" as part of His guidance in my life. When my spirit feels troubled or anxious, or when I don't have a sense of victory at a time when I should, I have learned to stop and pray. Or spend more time in reading the Word to be the light to my path. Perhaps the Lord is wanting me to wait and not get ahead of Him.

At other times, He might want to reveal something to me or give new instructions for me to follow. In those times when I am seeking direction, I will pray and ask Jesus to bring me some confirmation that I am going in the right direction. I have learned to trust that "inner witness' or those 'still' or 'troubled' waters in my spirit.

Isaiah 30:21 speaks of this sensitivity to the witness of the Lord. *"Your own ears will hear him. Right behind you a voice will say, "This is the way you should go," whether to the right or to the left"* (NLT). His guidance and confirmations will come through a variety of ways. But you can know that as you continue to be willing and obedient, His Spirit will continue to bear witness with your spirit throughout the process. Philippians 4:6-7 – *"Don't worry about anything; instead pray about everything. Tell God what you need and thank Him for all He has done. Then you will experience God's peace, which exceeds anything you can understand. His peace will guard your hearts and minds as you live in Christ Jesus"* (NLT).

Principle 3: *Trust God to complete it.*

Philippians 1:6 promises, *"And I am sure of this, that He who began a good work in you will bring it to completion at the day of Jesus Christ"* (ESV). Sometimes it is easier to start but not so easy to keep going. That is our walk of faith.

Hebrews 11:1 – *"Now faith is the assurance of things hoped for, the conviction of things not seen"* (ESV). Faith is needed when you can't see! Trust in God will be required before the final victory comes. Yet it is that very "trial of our faith" spoken of in I Peter 1:7 that is more precious than gold in God's sight. The journey of our selling and buying a house had many turns and twists. Some things seemed impossible, at other times it felt we were at an impasse. At every twist, turn or impasse, we had to continue following the specific instructions the Holy Spirit was giving to us.

I would be reminded about the Apostle Peter when he encountered Jesus walking on the water. Matthew 14:28-31 - And Peter answered him:

> *"Lord, if it is you, command me to come to you on the water." He said, "Come." So Peter got out of the boat and walked on the water and came to Jesus. But when he saw the wind, he was afraid, and beginning to sink he cried out, "Lord, save me." Jesus immediately reached out his hand and took hold of him, saying to him, "O you of little faith, why did you doubt?"* (ESV)

We have to choose to walk by faith, and then keep on walking. We have to trust God to not only bring us to it, but also bring us through it. In those moments of 'testing' on our journey, I knew I must not doubt! Psalms 9:10 - *"And those who know Your name put their trust in You, for You, O LORD, have not forsaken those who seek you"* (ESV). What a wonderful way to live life! I am forever thankful that we have learned, you don't need money. You just need God.

PRAYER

Lord, You are always so faithful. You not only care about meeting my needs, but you want me to have Your best. Thank you that I can always trust your guidance even when it doesn't make sense to me. Help me to wait on Your Holy Spirit to guide me and keep me always in step with You. In Jesus's name, Amen.

CHAPTER 7

Bank Error in Your Favor

Jaime Luce

The day had come. While holding my newborn, I just received the notice that the owners of the home we'd lived in happily for four years were moving back and going to live in the house we occupied. Every possible thought began running through my mind. We actually need more space and we've grown out of this home. But where do we go? How will I manage a move with a newborn and a toddler? Where will the kids go to school? Do we rent again, or do we buy? The questions were endless.

I immediately called my husband Joel. We didn't have time to waste. We took the evening to talk and pray about what to do. After praying, we felt that it was time to buy. This would take the Lord's intervention because aside from a couple of car loans, we had no real credit to speak of since this was our first buy. We had heard stories of how difficult it could be. The good news was that

I used to work for a moving company before we married. I understood what I needed to prepare for as far as the house was concerned. But that was not the problem. The problem was even if we found a house, we weren't prepared to pay a down payment. It was going to be a faith walk for sure.

We contacted a real estate agent to see what was available. We have always liked single-story ranch style homes. He told us there was a beautiful one for sale in the town where my grandparents used to live. From the minute we drove up, I thought it was perfect. It had the right number of bedrooms, an open style floor plan with a kitchen that was open to the den. It even had a huge master bathroom with two closets. It was a dream. Then, when we saw the price tag, we knew we were only dreaming.

We went home with the flyer in hand. Somehow this house was already in my heart even though it seemed impossible. I prayed and said, "Lord what do You say about this?" I heard in my spirit "anoint it with oil." I knew that meant I needed to pray and claim it as mine. I just knew He was setting it apart for us. How, I didn't know, and I didn't care. If He was saying yes, then I wanted that house.

I immediately ran to the kitchen to grab the olive oil. I opened the lid and poured some on my finger and anointed the picture of the house. Faith seemed to surge in me. I knew it was mine. Which is why I was shocked when the real estate agent contacted us and said someone had put an offer in and the homeowners accepted it. My heart about hit the floor. I didn't understand. I knew I had heard the Lord. I had what my family calls "the witness of the Spirit," which is an inner knowing in the deepest part of your being. So this didn't make any sense.

My husband said that we should just keep praying. I began to think that maybe the house would fall out of escrow. Besides, we didn't have the money so what was I thinking? The month passed and we got word that escrow did indeed close. We wouldn't get the house. But I just couldn't turn it loose. My spirit had a grip on it. We continued to pray knowing our time was running out. I then thought well maybe these new owners will have a job change and have to move. I think I thought of every crazy kind of scenario all the while believing that somehow this house would be mine.

A few weeks later, we received another call from the real estate agent. He said a house in that neighborhood had come on the market. Joel was at work since it was midweek, so I agreed to go meet him by myself. As I pulled up, I was immediately confused. The street name was different but there it was. My house! It was the exact same house. Then I quickly realized it was even better. It had a beautiful circular drive that was in addition to the garage drive. With a green belt, pigmy palms, and Iris flowers all in bloom. Surely, I was dreaming.

As we entered the home, I had to contain my excitement. The carpet and paint were the perfect color for our furniture. The backyard already had a huge swing set and slide. There was a very large grass area, an equally large, cemented area for bikes, skateboards, and the like. It even had a basketball hoop and large side yard. It was above and beyond what I was hoping for. I called Joel as quickly as I could and asked if he could leave work and meet us at the house. He said he could, and he came right over. Of course, he felt the same way I did. We loved it!

We went home and had a serious heart-to-heart with each other and then prayed together. I remember it like it was yesterday. We were sitting on our bed and Joel turned to me and said, "I think we should put in an offer." Forget the fact that we don't have any money. I didn't care in that moment. I just looked at him and like a child I said, "Really? Okay!" with a huge smile plastered on my face. He reached over for the phone and called the agent.

We did it! We made the offer. Now what? None of this made any sense in the natural. But like it is so many times with faith, it doesn't make sense. That's why you need faith.

The agent told us that he would call us when he had news. Waiting was torture. But then came the call. They accepted our offer. I flipped. I was so excited. My poor husband didn't know what to do with me. Don't misunderstand me. He was just as excited, but he was the one who would be responsible in the financial department. Though we had been building our credit we knew it wasn't substantial enough to buy this house.

I would normally not discuss personal finances but that is the point of this book and without knowing the magnitude you won't realize the power of God. With that said, the house was listed for $500,000.00. And that was in 1998. If we were going to buy this house, it would take God doing it. We needed a major miracle. You don't usually buy a large house right out of the gate. You buy a small starter house and work your way up. None of that seemed to matter. We believed this was our home. We prayed and spoke to the bank. To our shock, they went ahead and prequalified us for exactly $500,000.00. Miracle number one accomplished. The bigger problem now loomed. We needed $50,000.00 by close of escrow for our down payment.

That thirty days seemed to fly by. It was closing day of escrow, and the money needed to be turned into the escrow office by close of that day. As of that morning, we had none. I am not exaggerating. Joel was in sales. He always knew before his commission check what it should be. He told me that it won't be enough. If we didn't have enough, we would fall out of escrow. He went to work that day and received his check. He opened it up and to his utter shock, the check that was supposed to be for $25,000.00 read $50,000.00. He immediately called me and told me he didn't understand. He knew that couldn't be right. He went over all of his paperwork multiple times and said it doesn't make any sense.

I told him "I don't care how you got it. You better accept the handiwork of God and get down to that escrow office before they close." I was completely beside myself. I didn't know if I should jump, yell, or run around in circles. God did it! I don't know how He did it, but He did it! Joel took the check in, and we closed on our house. We were so anxious that literally we had a van packed and sitting in front of the house waiting while the previous owners were still getting the last of their things out. I told you I was good at moving, though I don't think they appreciated my skill.

After that weekend of move-in, Joel went to work on Monday. He went into the payroll department because he wanted to understand what happened that he received this check. After they looked everything over the payroll officer realized she had made a mistake. She had actually paid Joel double. She felt terrible and apologized for making the mistake saying, "We want to make this right. If it's okay with you, we will just take a little out of each subsequent paycheck until it is paid back." Joel thought "are you kidding me? Of course, I will let you do that." God orchestrated the big double payment so we could get into our house just in time. It was like playing monopoly and receiving the card that says, "bank error in your favor." What a miracle. Once again, we understood afresh that you don't need money. You just need God.

PLAY CALL: *Anoint, believe, and receive.*

Sometimes practically applying the Word of God can seem strange or even ridiculous. People like to let their rational minds overrule their spirits. But that's exactly all that's necessary to stay in the natural and out of the supernatural. If what we needed was naturally attainable then we wouldn't need the Lord at all. What we need is His super to take over our natural. Supernatural outcomes take supernatural measures. The Lord picks and empowers the method. He establishes the strategy. Our job is to believe He will do what He says He will do. Our part is to believe that our impossible has now become possible by the power of the One who instructed us. Our faith believes, regardless of the natural that surrounds us because we've deployed the supernatural. You are now positioned in the realm of more than enough, where you can receive all that you need.

ANOINT, BELIEVE AND RECEIVE
Bank Error in Your Favor

According to the *New Oxford American Dictionary*, to anoint literally means to smear or rub with oil. In the Bible, anointing was used on anything from the utensils used in the tabernacle to the offerings given, on the priests who served and Israel's kings. Anointing oil represents something that is being set apart. Just as your fingerprint is your personal mark, anointing oil is God's mark. It's a claiming of territory. Anointing holds power. Just as someone could use the king's signet ring as authority about a matter, so we use the anointing oil. It is the sign or signet of our King. Exodus 40:9 (NIV) says, *"Take the anointing oil and anoint the tabernacle and everything in it; consecrate it and all its furnishings, and it will be holy."* The act of anointing says you go from being ordinary to being consecrated or declared sacred. Here in lie the principles.

Principle 1: *Let God choose.*

As kids, we played a game called Red Rover. There were two opposing teams and a group of unclaimed people in the middle. Each team would have a chance to say, "Red Rover, Red Rover, "send _____ (fill in the blank with a person's name) right over." If you were in the middle, you hoped they would call your name. You wanted to be chosen. You wanted distinction. Anointing chooses. Not man. When I prayed and asked the Lord about the house, I had to understand that He may say, "Yes, that's the one" or "No, that isn't it." He chooses. He chose which articles were needed and to be used in the Tabernacle. He chose who would serve as the priests for His service, and He chose who would serve as king.

In 1 Samuel 16, this "choosing" is displayed.

> [1]*Now the Lord said to Samuel, "How long will you mourn for Saul, seeing I have rejected him from reigning over Israel? Fill your horn with oil and go; I am sending you to Jesse the Bethlehemite. For I have provided Myself a king among his sons."* [2]*And Samuel said, "How can I go? If Saul hears it, he will kill me." But the Lord said, "Take a heifer with you, and say, 'I have come to sacrifice to the Lord.'* [3]*Then invite Jesse to the sacrifice, and I will show you what you shall do; you shall anoint for Me the one I name to you."* [6]*So it was, when they came, that he looked at Eliab and said, "Surely the Lord's anointed is before Him!"* [7]*But the Lord said to Samuel, "Do not look at his appearance or at his physical stature, because I have refused him. For the Lord does not see as man sees; for man looks at the outward appearance, but the Lord looks at the heart."* [8]*So Jesse called Abinadab, and made him pass before Samuel. And he said, "Neither has the Lord chosen this one."* [9]*Then Jesse*

made Shammah pass by. And he said, "Neither has the Lord chosen this one." ¹⁰ Thus Jesse made seven of his sons pass before Samuel. And Samuel said to Jesse, "The Lord has not chosen these." ¹¹ And Samuel said to Jesse, "Are all the young men here?" Then he said, "There remains yet the youngest, and there he is, keeping the sheep." And Samuel said to Jesse, "Send and bring him. For we will not sit down till he comes here." ¹² So he sent and brought him in. Now he was ruddy, with bright eyes, and good-looking. And the Lord said, "Arise, anoint him; for this is the one!" ¹³ Then Samuel took the horn of oil and anointed him in the midst of his brothers; and the Spirit of the Lord came upon David from that day forward. So Samuel arose and went to Ramah.
(NKJV)

This beautiful example shows that God uses anointing oil to choose. He marks what He claims. The Lord told me to mark and claim that house as mine in the same way He marks and claims what's His. It is a spiritual outward symbol of a heavenly action. In heaven it was done. I was now expecting it to happen on earth. Matthew 16:19 says, *"And I will give you the keys of the kingdom of heaven, and whatever you bind on earth will be bound in heaven, and whatever you loose on earth will be loosed in heaven"* (NKJV). I was in essence "loosening" the home.

The anointing doesn't lie. The oil could not flow until it found what God had chosen. This is why we don't just anoint everything. As I pointed out earlier, God chooses the strategy. I don't anoint anything and everything. It's not my choice. It's God's. By allowing Him to choose, I am guaranteed the outcome. When God gave the command to anoint the tabernacle and the vessels, those things became holy. They no longer could be considered common. They must be treated differently and held in an uncommon regard because what God anoints, He watches over. I knew if God gave us that house, I didn't have to worry about it. God had it covered. He told me to anoint it. He had claimed it for me.

Principle 2: *Just Believe.*

1 Thessalonians 2:13 (NIV) says it this way, *"And we also thank God continually because, when you received the word of God, which you heard from us, you accepted it not as a human word, but as it actually is, the word of God, which is indeed at work in you who believe."* As Christians we believe the Word of God is the final say so. We don't regard what He says as human and changing. And when we believe it, it goes to work in us and for us.

Hebrews 11:6 says, *"But without faith it is impossible to please Him, for he who comes to God must believe that He is, and that He is a rewarder of those who diligently seek Him"* (NKJV). The book of James, chapter 1, says it this way.

⁶"But let him ask in faith, with no doubting, for he who doubts is like a wave of the sea driven and tossed by the wind. ⁷For let not that man suppose that he will receive anything from the Lord; ⁸he is a double-minded man, unstable in all his ways" (NKJV).

I had a choice that day. I heard that the home I had anointed sold to another buyer. In the natural you would just say I missed it on this one. Game over. Start again. But anointing it changed everything. I didn't choose to anoint it. The Lord did. I simply chose to believe the Lord. My faith had to be proven and most likely so will yours. We call it "a fight of faith" because there is a battle to be won. You will need to flex your faith muscles and, in many cases, grow them. Don't turn loose so quickly of what the Lord has spoken to you. Stand on that promise. Though David was anointed to be king that day, it would be many trying and painful years before it would come to pass.

In Genesis 37, we read about Joseph and his dreams. He was seventeen when God gave him dreams about his promised destiny. They did not come to pass until he was thirty years old. Speaking of Joseph, Psalms 105:19 says, *"Until the time that his word came to pass, the word of the Lord tested him"* (NKJV). Joseph was tested when he was put in a pit and sold into slavery. Then tested again when he was falsely accused and thrown in prison. The house I believed was mine was sold to another. Then, even when we saw it was still ours, we had to believe for the money we did not have. You can't let the test change your mind about what God said. Don't let what you see happen change what you know you heard.

Listen to what God says of Himself in the first part of Malachi 3:6, *"For I am the Lord, I do not change"* (NKJV), or Isaiah 55:11 *"So shall My word be that goes forth from My mouth; It shall not return to Me void, But it shall accomplish what I please, And it shall prosper in the thing for which I sent it"* (NKJV). And in Numbers 23:19 (NIV) we read, *"God is not human, that he should lie, not a human being, that he should change his mind. Does he speak and then not act? Does he promise and not fulfill?"*

Our God is faithful and true. *"For the Scripture says, whoever believes on Him will not be put to shame"* (Romans 10:11, NKJV). You can count on God!

Principle 3: *Receive.*

This may seem obvious, but it isn't. When God blesses, there will always be those voices, whether from within or without, that tell you, "You shouldn't be able to have this or that." Or "why should you be able to when others aren't able." "You don't need all that." "Is that really necessary?" Instead of receiving God's favor with joy, you could accept shame or misplaced guilt.

I'll never forget what I heard Bishop T.D. Jakes say when he taught about Joseph and his coat of many colors and how his father favored him. His brothers ridiculed, mocked, and despised him for that favor. But the

Bishop said, "If God gives you the coat, get you a matching hat baby, and wear it in style!"

I've heard it said that favor isn't fair. One of the reasons it isn't is because many times it takes faith and faithfulness to obtain that favor. A price many aren't willing to pay. But if you can believe it, you can receive it. Mark 9:23 tells us that *Jesus said to him, "If you can believe, all things are possible to him who believes"* (NKJV). Stay in the place of faith, and favor will grow. It was said of both John the Baptist and of Jesus, that they grew in favor with both God and man. And so can you. You can grow so close to the Author of every blessing that people won't understand how you are so blessed.

It made no sense for the payroll department to make such a huge error and then not expect to receive the check back. Instead, favor was at work. They apologized to us. They didn't ask for anything back. Instead, they made a way to rectify it in such a way that it was never a burden. That very act proved beyond doubt that we didn't need money. We just needed God. Had it not been God and instead just a mistake, we would have had to pay back the money in full, creating a whole new need and burden. What we needed was God. He gave us His favor and His blessing. There is no greater gift to receive than that. We received His great provision with joy, and you should too. Don't lose out because of false humility and reject the hand of God. Receive and be blessed.

PRAYER

Nothing is too difficult for you, Lord. You are able to do exceedingly and abundantly and above all that I could ask or ever imagine according to your promise in scripture. Though my needs are great. You, oh Lord, are greater. Share with me your strategies and methods. And help me follow your leading. In Jesus's name, Amen.

CHAPTER 8

Second Chances

Jaime Luce

I will start with a little background. Jeremy is the youngest in our family. There are seven years between us. I'm the oldest. My poor sister Jenny is stuck in the middle. The oldest is usually the protector which was absolutely true for me. I was like a little mother to Jeremy since he was so much younger than I was. This was often a problem for Jenny. It seemed to her that Jeremy could get away with anything as the baby. He was also the only boy which didn't help. Truth be told, she was right many times, but he was *the baby* after all.

Jeremy was in his teenage years when revival swept through the nation. Our church in Covina, California was also experiencing a revival. At that time, Jeremy had faithfully served in both the children's and youth departments under their respective leaders. Since January first of that year, nine months after graduating high school, Jeremy had been praying and asking the Lord for direction. Four months later, during one of the evening revival services, Jeremy prayed at the altar for two hours. It was at that altar that the Lord answered his prayer.

The answer was a call into full time ministry. The impact of the answer reverberated through Jeremy like lightning because this was not just the answer to a vocational question. This was an answer to his life's purpose and calling. He now not only knew what he was to do right now but what he was to do for the rest of his life. It was the answer to life's greatest question of "Why am I here?" Jeremy would be a pastor. He was so excited and so were we.

The plan was to begin interning at the church and begin Bible college. There was a Bible college very close by and though finances were tight our parents put the money together making a way for Jeremy to follow his call. It was a good beginning but sometimes college comes ready for us before we are ready for it. Jeremy wasn't quite disciplined enough being *the baby and all.* I say that a little tongue in cheek, but he really wasn't mature enough yet. It started with missed classes and then the inevitable happened, and Jeremy was dropped not realizing that was his one shot.

As time passed, Jeremy wrestled with the tug of his call weighing on his heart. He'd now been interning for three years. The question of "how long can I continue to intern?" troubled him. He had now grown up immensely and had a new healthy dose of perspective. He didn't know what to do. Now that he was ready for college, the money was gone. He knew now how it had been wasted and he couldn't change it. Time was slipping away while the need for a job now loomed. It seemed the broken plan could not be mended. He felt he had blown it and that he didn't deserve a second chance. He could only pray for God's intervention and mercy.

Then opportunities began to present themselves. The youth pastor with whom Jeremy had served under was now in Seattle and offered for him to come and be a pastor there. Outside of his parents, this man was the most influential person in Jeremy's life at that time and with whom he had a great relationship. The downside was he would need to find fulltime employment because the position was not paid.

Then, the church he'd grown up in, was currently attending, and interning for, told him they wanted to create a position for him where he could be used more. The exact job had not yet been threshed out, but it was an opportunity. Without college, Jeremy kept telling the Lord, "I'm not ready. I'm not ready." Yet in his prayer time, he heard the Lord say, "You are ready." But ready for what?

Jeremy wanted to follow the call of God on his life, but he just didn't have peace about either of these opportunities. The first offer was with not just a church but a close friend. In the natural, Jeremy wanted to do this. The second option would allow him to remain with family and friends which means the world to Jeremy. And neither of these opportunities would pay to get him back into Bible college. He realized he had blown it, and he deeply regretted wasting the opportunity he was given. Regret is such a thief. After stealing your yesterday, it keeps you paralyzed today, robbing you of your tomorrows.

It's hard enough when you know you should have done something differently not wasting a great opportunity. It's worse when you feel your purpose was wrapped up in that package you gave away so easily. It is the age-old story of Jacob and Esau. Esau gave his birthright away for a bowl of red beans and no amount of tears could bring it back to him.

In the same way, Mom and Dad could not fix this for Jeremy. They didn't have any more money to send him back to school. They had given him all they had, and now that was gone. It was no longer in their control.

One morning, Jeremy was sitting on the couch in the downstairs living room. My mom saw him there and could tell he was deeply discouraged. Up until this day, it seemed that Jeremy had vacillated back and forth about his plan forward and what he would do. Seeing his misery Mom decided it was time to cut to the chase. She went downstairs and looked Jeremy in the eye with all earnestness and asked him, "Jeremy, what do you *really* want to do?" Jeremy turned to her and said with all sincerity, "I want to go to Bible college."

She replied with the same wisdom given her from her mother as a child when she needed shoes. She said, "Well son, we don't have any more money for that. But if that really is God's will then you need to pray and ask God and God will make a way. If it's God's will then God will open the door."

Over the past several weeks at church, my mother had been teaching on the story in Luke chapter five, when Peter was called into the ministry. She had titled the message "God's got enough fish to sink your boat." Peter had been fishing all night and caught nothing. Jesus was there at the shore with a huge crowd hungry to hear what he would say. He saw Peter pulling in his nets with nothing to show for it. Jesus told Peter to let down his net again for a great catch, but Peter said, *"we've toiled all night and caught nothing. But, nevertheless, at your word I will let down the net"* (NKJV). When he did, they began catching so many fish that their nets were breaking. They had to motion to the boats nearby to help, filling both of their boats to overflowing. After this catch, Peter felt so unworthy that he asked the Lord to go away from him because he was a sinful man. Yet it was in this very condition that Jesus told him to follow Him, and He'd make him a fisher of men.

When my mom told Jeremy that they didn't have the money to help him, the Spirit brought this message to Jeremy's mind, and he humbly but in faith looked at her and quietly said, "God's got enough fish to sink my boat."

I find it no coincidence that this story about Peter following the call of Jesus on his life was the very story God brought up in Jeremy's spirit that day. Little did he know that God was about to sink his boat so he too could follow Him and the plan for his life so perfectly.

I am sure you have heard the statement "God's will, God's bill." It seems simple but there is truth in it. If God has a plan for you and you are willing to fulfill that plan, He will make a way even if there seems to be no way.

A couple of days after that conversation and much prayer, the phone rang. It was another opportunity from the pastor Jeremy had served under in the Children's ministry in Covina. They had moved and were now pastoring in Colorado at a church whose international ministry went all over the world and with great reputation. They wanted Jeremy to come and serve as the Children's pastor there. They knew Jeremy well. They knew his call and his giftings. They also knew he wanted and should go to Bible College. It just so happened that the church they served at had a Bible college. They would not only hire him as the children's pastor, which is a paid position, but pay for his tuition to attend the college.

Here was the dilemma. Jeremy didn't feel called to children's ministry. He felt his calling was youth ministry. He now had three opportunities. Which was God's choice? Talk about a lot of fish. There were so many fish that Jeremy needed help with what to do with them just like Peter.

That following Sunday Jeremy was weighted with the decision that needed to be made. After church he'd decided to go straight home. This was unusual for him, but he needed to pray. On the way home, what rose up in his spirit was the phrase, "This is too good of an opportunity to pass up." He knew it was in regard to Colorado.

When my parents arrived home, my mother said to Jeremy, "Son, I just want to share with you what we as your family feel about your decision. It's your life and your calling. We just want you know what we are feeling in our spirits. Today, at lunch together with your aunt and uncle and your grandmother we just felt that *this is too good of an opportunity to pass up.*" It was the exact phrase that the Lord spoke to Jeremy driving home.

God is so good. He had done it again. He just sank Jeremy's boat. And that's just like God. He confirmed His call on Jeremy's life by opening this opportunity and paid the bill. God had not changed his mind nor his plan. He had not revoked His call or held back his goodness. He covered Jeremy's misstep with His amazing grace. He gave him a second chance. Jeremy would both go to Bible College and serve fulltime in the ministry. Jeremy had just learned for himself in a huge way that *you don't need money. You just need God.*

PLAY CALL: *Repent and accept.*

Whether intentionally or unintentionally, we all fall. We have a mistaken notion that if we fall having known the truth, we are now disqualified. You would never condemn a baby for falling. In fact, a child's brain is wired in such a way that the fall teaches them what to do right the next time so that they don't continually fall. Their muscles remember the movements and grow stronger. They may wabble a bit while learning to remain balanced, but they are learning. That may seem over simplified, but the essence of the fall is the same. When we fall, the One teaching us lifts us back up, dusts us off and urges us to have another go at it. We are told not to make the same mistake twice but rather learn from it so that we do not fall in the same way again. That is the advantage of falling as a Christian. The fall doesn't have to be final. Proverbs 24:16 says, *"For a righteous man may fall seven times and rise again, but the wicked shall fall by calamity"* (NKJV). The mercy of God is so deep and wide that your misstep will still be inbounds. You are still within reach of the Lords outstretched arms. Though we don't deserve it He stands ready to redeem. Lamentations 3:22-23 says, *"Because of the Lord's great love we are not consumed, for his compassions never fail. They are new every morning; great is your faithfulness"* (NIV). His desire is always to restore and to make the way for us. He simply needs us to accept his invitation to pick us back up and put us in the right place.

REPENT AND ACCEPT
Second Chances

Many people compare themselves to the disciple Peter. Why is that? I think it's because we all know about Peter's failures. We identify with his faults. He was the one who would shoot off with his mouth and then have to eat his words. He was the one who would cut off a man's ear and need Jesus to clean up his mess. But what I love about Peter is he is also the first to jump out of the boat in faith. He dared to walk on water when no one else came close. Don't be discouraged. Big faith can also be akin to big falls. The failures are not a measuring rod of your ability nor are they a picture of what's ahead.

You may be thinking, "But you don't know what I've done." Or "but I knew better. I deliberately did it." I am certain this is exactly what Peter said. Jesus told Peter the night of his arrest in Matthew 26:34 (NIV) *"Truly I tell you," Jesus answered, "this very night, before the rooster crows, you will disown me three times."* The King James version says, "deny me," but it went much deeper than that. To deny is to reject but to disown is personal. Jesus was saying you are going to completely disown me and not just once but three times. Not only did Peter do this, but he did it when Jesus needed him the most. One minute he is defending Jesus and willing to die while swinging his sword. The next minute he is swearing he never knew Him. Let's learn from the principles found in Peters fall.

Principle 1: *Humble yourself.*

In Matthew chapter twenty-six, the disciples get into an argument about who is the greatest. Jesus teaches them that in order to be great you must first be the servant of all. He told them to follow His example of serving even to the washing of their feet. Proverbs 16:18 tells us that pride comes before a fall, so Peter's fall was inevitable because he was struggling with pride.

Pride is deceptive. It keeps you from seeing your blind spot and dulls your hearing. Jesus saw the trouble coming and tried to warn Peter in v.31 when He said, *"Simon, Simon, behold, Satan demanded to have you, that he might sift you like wheat, 32 but I have prayed for you that your faith may not fail. And when you have turned again, strengthen your brothers."* But Peter didn't hear the warning. Instead, he said in v.33 *"Though they all fall away because of you, I will never fall away."* (ESV).

Then in the garden Jesus had to correct Peter again. The book of John tells us that it was Peter who had used his sword to cut off the ear of the high priests' servant.

Jesus told Peter to put away his sword and then healed the servant's ear. This event triggered embarrassment and shame for Peter. When he relied on his own unction and strength, he failed. And this failure was public and in front of both friends and foes.

Pride doesn't want to be exposed, so it runs and hides. Peter ran away and tried to hide from what was happening. And pride will do the same to you. You might be so ashamed that you do as Peter did and begin denying that you ever even knew Jesus. You might even disown him. But don't lose hope. Jesus saw Peter watching from a distance and He sees you. He still has a plan for you and a way to bring it to pass.

Principle 2: *Accept forgiveness.*

To humble yourself is to repent. One of the biblical definitions of repentance means to turn or return. After Jesus's resurrection, in Mark 16:1-8, an angel told Mary and Salome to go tell Jesus's disciples "and Peter" that He wasn't there. He had risen and would meet them in Galilee. When Peter heard this news, he had a decision to make. He could remain in self-pity, or he could accept the invitation to return. This is why we love Peter. As soon as he heard that Jesus was not in the tomb, he ran. But this time he ran to see Jesus and not from Him. He had emptied himself of his pride and returned with all of his heart.

To return is to accept the call from Jesus. It doesn't matter what you've done or failed to do. Jesus offers forgiveness and calls your name. This call reminds us of what Jesus told Peter when He warned him in Matthew 26:32 *"but I have prayed for you that your faith may not fail. And when you have turned again, strengthen your brothers"* (ESV). Look at the amazing thing Jesus has done here. He not only forgives. He restores. Jesus didn't make Peter go to the back of the line. He didn't demote him. He told him to go back and take his place among his brethren and to strengthen them.

For my brother Jeremy, God not only got him into school, but he also put him directly into the pastorate and with pay. Jesus doesn't partially forgive or partially restore. He completes what He started. Philippians 1:6 says, *"being confident of this very thing, that He who has begun a good work in you will complete it until the day of Jesus Christ"* (NKJV). He is the author and the finisher of our faith according to Hebrews 12:2.

Principle 3: *Go for it!*

My brother Jeremy could have walked away from the call of God on his life forever. He could have thought that he'd blown it so why should he get another chance. And he could have never dared to believe that God would make a way where there seemed to be no way. Peter could have decided that he wasn't worthy to return to or desire his place back among his brethren. In both cases, had they not returned in humility and accept the call, lives would have been lost forever.

Peter and the disciples gave us the New Testament. They turned the world upside down. My brother is a Pastor who teaches the word of God and has brought many into the Kingdom of God, saving them from eternal damnation. Your testimony is just as powerful. It is just as important. And God will make a way for you. Even today, if you will not let disappointment or pride hold you back, you can see God do the impossible with your life. The decision is yours. God has already made the plan and made the provision. He just needs you.

My brother Jeremy thought he needed money to get back on the road God had carved out for him. Peter thought he had to go back to his old job of fishing. Both thought their opportunity to follow God's call was gone. And it would have been, *but God!* My husband, Joel, used to always say, "I'm going to preach a sermon someday on all the "buts" in the Bible." Meaning God's people were always facing impossible circumstances, but God would do the impossible and change everything.

I find it ironic and just like God that my brother received a "call" from his old pastor which set in motion the plan God had for his life. Peter received the "call" from the women who went to the tomb that day. Hebrews 3:15 tells us that in the day we hear His voice, or "call," not to harden our hearts. Don't choose to stay stuck.

Your heavenly Father is always there, watching with open arms when you decide to return. He will make the way and He will provide the way. You will find out like Jeremy that *you don't need money. You just need God.*

PRAYER

Thank you, Lord, for picking me up when I fall. I thank you that you don't leave me in my circumstance. When I'm in a pit of my own digging or at the hands of another, you see to it that I am brought out safely and my feet are planted on solid ground. I declare today, "God's got enough fish to sink my boat." I turn back to you today for your direction and instruction. Lead me into the plan you have for my life. In Jesus's name, Amen.

CHAPTER 9

It's In the Trade Show

Jaime Luce

I was sitting on the couch in my aunt's living room reading my Bible. I could see Joel walking up the walkway through the picture window. As soon as I let him in, he asked if we could sit down to talk about something. He had a worried look on his face. We sat on the couch facing one another. "I'm thinking about quitting my job" he said. "I make enough money to take care of myself but not enough to support a wife and two children."

We were not yet engaged so he was worried what I would think. He explained that he had prayed and told the Lord he wanted to be able to marry me. He asked the Lord to provide a better paying job in order to support me and the kids. He told me about a dream he'd had the night before after praying where he clearly heard the words "Daniel 10." Not sure if this was the Lord speaking or just a late dinner, he got up to write it down. The next morning, he grabbed his Bible and began to read.

He couldn't believe his eyes. It says:

> *¹In the third year of Cyrus king of Persia a thing was revealed unto Daniel, whose name was called Belteshazzar; and the thing was true, but the time appointed was long: and he understood the thing and had understanding of the vision. ² In those days I Daniel was mourning three full weeks." ³ I ate no pleasant bread, neither came flesh nor wine in my mouth, neither did I anoint myself at all, till three whole weeks were fulfilled.* (KJV)

God immediately had Joel's full attention because Cyrus was Joel's current boss's name. He was also Persian. He marveled that God would be speaking that specifically to him right out of the Bible. This passage and the subsequent portion tell of how Daniel prayed and fasted for twenty-one days in search of understanding and then receiving an answer. God sent an angel to bring the answer and tell him of things to come. This seemed to Joel to be an obvious and overt instruction from the Lord regarding the prayer he had prayed. He was going to begin a twenty-one day fast where he would eat no bread, no meat, and nothing sweet or pleasing, just as Daniel did. God seemed to be saying that if it worked for Daniel, it would work for him too. He then asked me what I thought.

I told him I absolutely thought it was the Lord. I had been on a fast when Joel and I met. This was one of the ways that the Lord often used to lead me into answers. He was so relieved. He thought that I would be upset thinking he was irresponsible to consider quitting a perfectly good job. He decided to wait to see how the Lord would instruct him after his fasting was finished.

Without delay, Joel began his fast. It was day fourteen when he had another dream like the first. In this dream he heard the phrase, "It's in the trade show." Again, this woke him up. He wrote it down on the pad of paper he had sitting on his bedside table and wondered what it meant. "It's in the trade show." He felt like he was living a scene out of *Field of Dreams* with an "If you build it, they will come." message. What in the world does this mean? What's in the trade show? Maybe a good lead, a new sale, or some new connection. Maybe a promotion. Maybe this meant absolutely nothing, and it was just a dream. After mulling it over, he remembered that he was scheduled to attend a trade show the following month. He didn't know what to expect but thought maybe something would occur while he was there.

The day of the tradeshow came. Though Joel went with anticipation, he was met with great disappointment. The trade show came and went without even as much as a whisper. Nothing. Not even a lead. This was all so confusing. Joel wondered if he had heard right.

Did it mean anything at all? He had completed his fast but, as of yet, nothing had changed. Was he wrong about the whole thing?

Several months went by. No answer came. Finances were no better, and it seemed that the fast had not produced anything. January rolled around. He was scheduled for another trade show. At this point Joel wasn't thinking about the fast or the cryptic dream. He attended with no real expectation.

When he arrived, his booth was positioned directly next to a booth belonging to a company called ABG. The sales manager there had struck up a conversation with Joel. After talking for a while, the man asked how much commission Joel made on what he sold. When he heard Joel's response, he told him that if he came to work for them, he would make twice as much selling the exact same amount. The sales manager said, "You should come by our facility and check us out." Then Joel remembered the dream. "It's in the trade show." Could this be what God had planned and he simply hadn't understood God's timing? Excited about the prospect, Joel said, "Alright, I'm actually going to play golf on Friday. I'll come by after that."

Friday morning came. It was a nice day for golf. Joel was playing a decent game until the thirteenth hole. To his own shock and amazement, he hit a hole-in-one! Now Joel is a decent golfer, but he is no Tiger Woods. He was so excited. He couldn't believe it. He said he knew better than to tell anyone in the clubhouse or they would expect him to buy drinks for everyone. The Lord knows he wasn't up for that nonsense! But what a good start to a great day. What he didn't know was that this was only the first act to a well-scripted, predestined day. A truly great day!

While still on that high and feeling pretty good, Joel began the drive to ABG. Still in his golf shorts, the sales manager welcomed him and gave him a tour, introducing him to several people throughout the warehouse and all their facilities. While on the tour of the offices, the owner, an old gruff Italian man, saw Joel and quipped, "Is this how you come dressed for an interview?" Joel retorted a little smugly, "Interview? I'm not here to be interviewed. I'm here to check you out."

Just then Joel noticed an old putter in the corner of the owner's office. He asked the owner if he played golf and said, "I just hit a hole-in-one this morning on the thirteenth hole at Azuza Greens Golf Course." To which the owner answered, "In all my years of playing golf, I have never hit a hole-in-one." He was so impressed, that he swung around and said, "Hire that kid." So, they did. The sales manager made the offer that day. Joel would be paid twice what he was making at his current job.

God had set him up. His fasting wasn't for nothing. The Lord had heard Joel's prayer. And in answering it, seemed to give His blessing for us to marry. God alone knew where the extra money was and led him right to it. He had ordered his steps and even his booth placement at the tradeshow.

Through asking, fasting and dreams, the Lord was teaching Joel that "You don't need money. You just need God."

PLAY CALL: *Ask, fast, and align.*

As believers, we are often the most reluctant to ask. James 4:2 (NKJV) strongly describes this lack. It says, *"You lust and do not have. You murder and covet and cannot obtain. You fight and war. Yet you do not have because you do not ask."* The NLT says it this way. *"You want what you don't have, so you scheme and kill to get it. You are jealous of what others have, but you can't get it, so you fight and wage war to take it away from them. Yet you don't have what you want because you don't ask God for it."* We think it is somehow wrong or selfish to ask for what we want. Not only is it not wrong to ask but it is necessary. The best decisions in life are made because someone asked the right questions. Without asking questions, understanding is limited if not stunted. To ask is to say either I don't know, or I don't have. It's a sign of humility. You lay down your will and pride and ask the One who knows. In Joel's case, asking led to fasting. Fasting led to proper spiritual hearing and alignment. Fasting humbles your flesh so your flesh can't get in the way of the right answer. It makes way for easy hearing and leading from the Lord, putting you in the right place at the right time.

ASK AND FAST
It's in the Trade Show

John 16:24 says, *"Until now you have asked nothing in My name. Ask, and you will receive, that your joy may be full"* (NKJV).

The scriptures are full of accounts where Jesus healed those who were sick. But there is one account where Jesus made the man ask for what he wanted. Mark 10:46-52 says,

> [46] *"Now they came to Jericho. As He went out of Jericho with His disciples and a great multitude, blind Bartimaeus, the son of Timaeus, sat by the road begging.* [47] *And when he heard that it was Jesus of Nazareth, he began to cry out and say, "Jesus, Son of David, have mercy on me!"* [48] *Then many warned him to be quiet; but he cried out all the more, "Son of David, have mercy on me!"* [49] *So Jesus stood still and commanded him to be called. Then they called the blind man, saying to him, "Be of good cheer. Rise, He is calling you."* [50] *And throwing aside his garment, he rose and came to Jesus.* [51] *So Jesus answered and said to him, "What do you want Me to*

do for you?" The blind man said to Him, "Rabboni,
that I may receive my sight." ⁵² Then Jesus said to
him, "Go your way; your faith has made you well."
And immediately he received his sight and followed
Jesus on the road. (NKJV)

This passage is a beautiful example of how Jesus in-
teracts with us and how He wants to specifically answer
our requests. Scripture tells us that He knows what we
need before we ask. So why make Bartimaeus say what
he wanted? The answer to this question leads to powerful principles we can all apply.

Principle 1: *Ask for what you want.*

Jesus knew what Bartimaeus needed but he required
him to ask. *So Jesus answered and said to him, "What do you*
want Me to do for you?" The blind man said to Him, "Rabbo-
ni, that I may receive my sight" (NKJV). Why did Jesus ask
him this? Jesus is so personal and intentional that it was
necessary for Bartimaeus to know himself what he really needed. Would he ask for money? After all he was
begging for money when Jesus called him to Him. Or
did he want to see?

We will all face this question when asking from the
Lord. Do you just think you need more money or are you
in need of something else? Joel thought he needed more
money. What he really needed was a divine connection

that would lead to a different job. He needed to be in the right place at the right time. And he wanted to be able to get married. God knew all of this. Human nature doesn't like to ask. We hear people say things like, "God knows where I am. He knows what I need so why doesn't He just do it?" The truth is God is wanting to teach us that what we really need is Him.

This blind man had just made a huge commotion to get Jesus's attention. He must have thought Jesus wouldn't pay attention to him personally. Even the disciples told him to be quiet. But Jesus wanted to give him both what he wanted and what he needed. Like the passage above, Jesus wanted Bartimaeus's joy to be full.

After he was healed, Jesus said, "Go your way; your faith has made you well" (NKJV). Bartimaeus not only received his healing, but he now had a relationship with Jesus. He now had faith. What was his faith? It was twofold. First, he believed that if he cried out then Jesus would hear him. And second, that he would receive what he asked for. With his eyesight, he no longer needed to beg. His financial need was also met. He could now work and make a living free from begging. We can have this same kind of faith. A faith that knows Jesus hears, and He answers. It's not a faith in faith, but faith in the One who can make the blind to see.

Principle 2: *Fast. Why fast?*

To understand this, we must look at how we were intended to live this life and make our decisions. We are three-part beings created spirit, soul (our mind, will and emotions), and body. We are first a spirit. We have a soul, and we live in a body. As Christians, we have gone from a dead spirit to a spirit that is alive. This is why we say we have been born again. If you are not born again, your spirit remains dead. Without a spirit made alive by Christ, who rules and reigns in your life, you are a dead spirit by default. Your soul is then being led by a body.

This is described by Jesus to Nicodemus in John 3:1-6.

> *[1]There was a man of the Pharisees named Nicodemus, a ruler of the Jews. [2]This man came to Jesus by night and said to Him, "Rabbi, we know that You are a teacher come from God; for no one can do these signs that You do unless God is with him." [3]Jesus answered and said to him, "Most assuredly, I say to you, unless one is born again, he cannot see the kingdom of God." [4]Nicodemus said to Him, "How can a man be born when he is old? Can he enter a second time into his mother's womb and be born?" [5]Jesus answered, "Most assuredly, I say to you, unless one is born of water and the Spirit, he cannot enter the kingdom of God. [6]That which is born of the flesh is flesh, and that which is born of the Spirit is spirit." (NKJV)*

Scripture often refers to the body and its carnal nature as the flesh. Flesh can only bring forth more flesh. It will demand and push for its way. When your flesh is in control, you won't ask the Lord for his intervention or direction. Instead, you will waste time and energy creating more needs instead of solving them. Abraham and Sarah learned this the hard way.

Genesis 16:1-4 says,

> *¹Now Sarai, Abram's wife, had borne him no children. And she had an Egyptian maidservant whose name was Hagar. ² So Sarai said to Abram, "See now, the Lord has restrained me from bearing children. Please, go into my maid; perhaps I shall obtain children by her." And Abram heeded the voice of Sarai. ³ Then Sarai, Abram's wife, took Hagar her maid, the Egyptian, and gave her to her husband Abram to be his wife, after Abram had dwelt ten years in the land of Canaan. ⁴ So he went into Hagar, and she conceived. And when she saw that she had conceived, her mistress became despised in her eyes.* (NKJV)

Sarai allowed herself to be led by her emotions. She grew impatient and came up with a plan birthed out of her flesh. But flesh only gives birth to flesh. So, Ishmael was born. Instead of waiting on the words God had spoken, they let their flesh take over. Their flesh didn't give them what God had intended for them or what they really wanted. They were promised a son of their union. Their plan backfired. Instead of being what they wanted, what they got mocked God's plan and it will do the same to you.

Genesis 21:8-9 *"So the child grew and was weaned. And Abraham made a great feast on the same day that Isaac was weaned. And Sarah saw the son of Hagar the Egyptian, whom she had borne to Abraham, scoffing."* (NKJV)

Living according to the flesh gets us out of order. As a Christian, we should live spirit, soul, and body. Our spirit should rule over our fleshly emotions, and our body should simply follow directions. Not the other way around.

Fasting corrects this. It demands that our spirit come into its proper place. It rules instead of being ruled. Fasting declares that Jesus is on the throne and not king stomach. If you have ever fasted, you will realize very quickly how much control your flesh exerts over you and your decisions. Flesh likes to be coddled. It is demanding and selfish. It is never satisfied and never relents.

For example, think about what happens when you get very hungry. Your stomach starts to burn and growl. Feeding it becomes priority number one. The body demands that the soul and its emotions get involved. You get a little out of sorts. You can't concentrate. You begin making decisions to feed your hunger. Your emotions will soon show who is in control. Instead of that healthy sensible meal, you're headed to the nearest drive thru. The only criterion is which one of them is the closest. Your "hangry" and short-tempered self begins to emerge.

Fasting strips your flesh of control. It causes your natural flesh man to bow and humble itself before the Lord, allowing for your spirit to come back into headship. It is from this humble position of fasting that the flesh is silenced, and you can more easily hear the still small voice of the Lord. It is this sacrifice that demands heavens attention. Fasting says, it is more important for me to hear the Lord than it is to eat. He is what I need. Like Peter, we say that the Lord alone has "the words of life" (John 6:68).

Scripture says, "when you fast," not "if you fast." Matthew 6:16 (NKJV) *"Moreover, when you fast, do not be like the hypocrites, with a sad countenance. For they disfigure their faces that they may appear to men to be fasting. Assuredly, I say to you, they have their reward."* It is expected that we would fast. In fact, there were those who asked Jesus why his disciples didn't fast. He answered them in Mark 2:19-20 saying, [19]*"And Jesus said to them, "Can the friends of the bridegroom fast while the bridegroom is with them? As long as they have the bridegroom with them they cannot fast.* [20]*But the days will come when the bridegroom will be taken away from them, and then they will fast in those days"* (NKJV). We are living in those days. Jesus, in essence, describes the purpose and remedy of fasting. Having Jesus physically present meant you had no need to fast. The remedy then to His physical absence in our need is fasting. It brings Him into the problem as the answer.

Though fasting is not easy, its benefits far outweigh the cost. We will all face problems in this life, but we have been given a way to access the heart of God and receive the help and intervention we desire from Him. The use of fasting will affect your relationship with the Lord on a very deep level. For Joel, fasting brought about a spiritual sensitivity and alertness to the plans and thoughts that God had toward him. His hope and faith were ignited. And yours will be too. The very process will increase your faith and develop your relationship with Him, giving you the confidence to ask for what you want and what you need.

Principle 3: *Align.*

If God has the answers, being able to hear Him is essential to following His leads and hearing those answers without the interference of the flesh. Your flesh wants to control. A fast corrects this order. Instead of being body, soul, and spirit you change the order by denying your flesh. You demand that your life and decisions line up as intended: spirit, soul, and body. From this order you prepare yourself to ask and hear an answer to your request.

Science has shown that when someone is missing one of their senses, the others are heightened and work at a higher and sharper level. This is what fasting does for our spirits. Losing the satisfaction and dominance of the body, causes your spirit to be sharpened. Your spiritual eyes and ears work more acutely. This gives you the advantage for hearing the direction and instructions God is giving you.

Joel asking for God's intervention came in the form of prayer and fasting. Without more money, he couldn't see a way forward. Spiritually speaking, his eyesight was dull, and he couldn't see. He also needed his hearing opened. Fasting caused his sense of spiritual hearing to increase even while he slept. Through this powerful tool of fasting, Joel was able to hear of a future intended plan that God had prepared for him, encouraging him to see an answer for his tomorrow.

The effects of fasting can have many different outworking's. In Joel's case, it caused him to be aware of the Lord's intentions which positioned him. It properly aligned him. This alignment of spirit first prompted him to receive heavenly dreams. Specifically, two separate dreams. Normally, Joel does not have dreams like this. But by fasting, Joel's ears were enabled to hear the wavelength of heaven and what God was saying. The dream then positioned him for the answer he was seeking. It gave him faith for the future that God was doing something on his behalf. It positioned him physically at a tradeshow to meet the right people. It even symbolically aligned him perfectly enough to hit a hole-in-one at the golf course, giving him favor with the owner.

Fasting is an outward sign of an inward surrender. Elisabeth Elliot, missionary and author, said, "To pray, 'thy will be done,' I must be willing, if the answer requires it, that my will be undone." Fasting surrenders the will so that God can have His way. He may answer you with a change of course or stay the course but He will answer you. He cares about what you want, and he knows what you need.

You may be like blind Bartimaeus, sitting and begging and hoping to scrape by. You may have dreams for your future or not have enough money to move forward like Joel. No matter what you want or need, let me remind you: You don't need money. You just need God. Jesus is always the answer. So, what are you waiting for? ASK!

PRAYER

Heavenly Father, you are the source of everything that is. I'm sorry for not coming to you first and relying only on myself. You desire to see me flourish and live the purpose you have put inside of me. Thank you for making a way where there seems to be no way. Thank you for caring about what concerns me. I ask you now to meet my need. I trust that you will make sure that I am in the right place at the right time because you are always faithful. In Jesus's name, Amen.

CHAPTER 10

Making God Connections

Judy Mercer

It was such a confusing time in our lives. The test of faith that would rock us to our core. We had never before faced a storm of this magnitude in our home. Unchartered waters can feel treacherous! The year was 1980.

My husband, Jim, co-owned a tire and wheel business in El Monte, California during the late 1970's. We now had three kids and I was working a full-time job. We had moved to a new home in Diamond Bar and life was in a happy place. Things felt so steady and secure – just the way I like it. His business was growing, and he was working hard. With having several of the top car dealerships and RV franchises in Southern California as their go-to source for upgraded tires and rims, we were feeling the winds of success. Then it happened! The storm came at us full force. The economic recession hit and hit us hard. Gas buying was limited to odd and even days, with gas lines hours long. Needless to say, no one, and I mean no one was upgrading their tires and wheels. Several of our RV franchises closed their doors overnight and when their employees arrived for work in the morning, they found padlocks on the gates. Our accounts receivables suffered along with them. We felt like we were circling the drain. We were stretched as thin as it could get. Would we even survive, or would we lose everything? We didn't know what to do. Jim's partner was then offered a good paying job, and we encouraged him to take it. We knew we didn't both need to suffer, and it might get even worse. But what was God's will for us? What should we do? Oh, how we prayed! Desperate times provoke desperate praying and that we did!

Jim has always been the steady one whose faith in God never wavers. I affectionately call him 'Father Abraham' because he just believes God will do what He says He will do and that's it. He refuses to entertain one ounce of fear. Finally, one evening Jim came through the front door with a look of determination on his face. Throwing his keys down on the kitchen counter, he announced to me the direction he felt led to take. He said he was going to run a small ad in the paper for only three days to sell the business. If the business sold in that three-day period, then that's what we would do – sell it. If it did not sell in that three-day window, we would take out a loan on our house and go even deeper in debt, but trust that it was God's will for us. That's exactly what he did. Through that small ad during that three-day period, a buyer contacted Jim and made a full price offer on the business with the caveat that Jim was to stay on for one year, at his full draw pay, and teach him the business. Jim agreed and for one year we were steady and secure again – just the way I like it.

But then the year ended. Now there was no job at all. And no doors for our future had opened. For the first time in his life Jim had to draw unemployment. But we knew that couldn't last forever. I would be emotionally okay all week long but once the weekend came, I cried all weekend long. This went on for weeks.

I will never forget the day we hit rock bottom. It was a beautiful Southern California spring day. Sunshine was spilling through the windows, the kids were outside playing, and it seemed like a normal laid-back Saturday morning. We were both sitting in our family room, Jim in his usual favorite "Dad" chair, with me on my rattan couch with its rust floral pattern cushions, matching draperies, and custom wall coverings. Usually, it's my favorite spot because it was just the way I like it. But on this Saturday morning none of that brought us the usual comfort and relaxation. We were both trying to pray but were so discouraged that no words were coming from our mouths. Jim was sitting with his head in his hands – which was a rare sight indeed. I was just crying and had no words either. We were so confused as to why this was happening to us since we always lived our lives for God, sought His will in everything, and always prayed about everything. We began searching our hearts, wondering if we had done something wrong to displease the Lord? Was this His discipline? Was God angry with us? Had we been disobedient somewhere and now the heavens were shut?

At that moment the Lord spoke directly to my heart. "This is *not* God. God will *never* put more on you than you can bear. *This is knocking you to your knees!*" I knew in that instant that if it wasn't God then it was the enemy – Satan – and we could fight and win this battle! When that revelation hit my spirit, I jumped up and with tears of joy and told Jim what God had just said. Those words hit Jim's spirit as well, and he stood up with hands raised to heaven, and we both began praising God and worshipping the Lord. Peace filled both of our hearts. The crying stopped. We just experienced a breakthrough, and we knew God was in control!

That following Monday when I came home from the office, Jim told me about what happened in his prayer time that morning. He said God had spoken specifically to him that "someone he knew, was going to introduce him to someone, who would introduce him to someone else who was going to hire him!" He went on to say, "Sounds crazy, doesn't it?" But he knew he had heard from God. Within a matter of days, a very close friend of Jim's, who had ministered with him in the Gospel music field, called and asked how things were. Once Jim told him his situation, his friend told him to get his resume together as he wanted to introduce him to someone, he knew in the automotive industry who was looking to hire. Jim put his resume together, showered, got cleaned up, and his friend came and picked him up. They both went to meet the contact. When Jim showed this contact his resume, which revealed that his gifts and talents had been in classic car restoration, and he had a special skill as a metal finisher which was fast becoming a lost art, as well as being a painter and craftsman, the contact responded by saying, "You don't want to work for me. I need to take you down the street to meet the owner. He would be very interested in what you can do." Little did Jim know that this 'other man' owned a huge corporation, and this body shop was just a side hobby because he had always had a vision to create a classic car restoration franchise.

After reading Jim's resume, he looked up at him and said, "Can you really do all these things?" Jim answered, "Yes." With that he proceeded to lead Jim out across the deep property to a large, expansive warehouse and there tucked away in the very back corner sat a 1955 Chevy hard top, totally stripped, sitting on four five-gallon drums. He turned to Jim and said, "Can you cut out the rusty body parts, metal finish it, and make it like new again?" Again, Jim said, "Yes." The gentleman proceeded to inquire exactly how he would do it, asking what the procedures would be and finally what equipment he would need. Jim walked him through the process he would take and what would be needed to complete it. Jim cautioned him that it would take time and a lot of money, to which he responded, "Money is no issue. How soon can you start?" They went back to the owner's office, discussed salary and all the equipment that Jim would need, and Jim was to start work the following Monday!

When Jim came home that evening and shared with me what had happened, well I have to say I was less than enthusiastic. As a young wife and mother of three children, telling me he had ONE car to fix brought me no sense of security at all. It sure didn't appear to be a long-term job, let alone a career move. Yet, I couldn't deny that "someone Jim knew, had introduced him to someone, who introduced him to someone else who hired him!" It had happened just the way the Lord had said to Jim in prayer. Again, peace came over me, and I knew this had to be God.

The next Monday Jim presented the owner with his complete layout of how he would begin to build the restoration business and all the equipment and supplies needed to get it off the ground. Over the next three months Jim was handed one blank check after another, and Classic Motor Cars was born. The business grew into a full restoration shop with Jim hiring fifteen car specialists and turning out show-winning cars for the next twenty-one years! We saw so many blessings in our lives during this time and experienced God's faithfulness over and over again.

God had totally created a job for us in answer to our desperate prayers. We had no money ourselves to ever start a business, but we quickly learned, *you Don't Need Money. You Just Need God.* God can create everything you need to provide for your life and the life of your family. If you will look to Him and His will.

PLAY CALL: *God is your creator!*

What doesn't exist is not out of reach. It is not final. Just because you don't have it now doesn't mean you won't have it. Every miracle in the Bible started with a problem. And if you have a problem, your God has a miracle. He is the creative God who creates something out of nothing. Jeremiah 32:27 (ESV) says, *"Behold, I am the LORD, the God of all flesh. Is anything too hard for me?"* Jeremiah 32:17 (ESV) reads, *"Ah, Lord GOD! It is you who have made the heavens and the earth by your great power and by your outstretched arm! Nothing is too hard for you."* Knowing that God is your creator should fill you with hope and faith. When we didn't have a source of income, God knew how to create the very thing we needed. When our hands could not create for ourselves, God's creative power caused a business to be birthed out of nothing. Romans 2:11 (ESV) tells us, *"For God shows no partiality."* How wonderful! What He does for one, He will do for **everyone** who puts their faith in Him and prays to Him in faith.

GOD IS YOUR CREATOR
Making God Connections

Principle 1: *You can be in the perfect will of God and still encounter a vicious storm!*

Just because the circumstances seem contrary to you doesn't mean you won't achieve all you have set out to accomplish.

Mark 4:35-40 (ESV) tells us *"On that day, when evening had come, he (Jesus) said to them, 'Let us go across to the other side.' And leaving the crowd, they took him with them in the boat, just as he was. And other boats were with him. And a great windstorm arose, and the waves were breaking into the boat, so that the boat was already filling. But he was in the stern, asleep on the cushion. And they woke him and said to him, "Teacher, do you not care that we are perishing?" And he awoke and rebuked the wind and said to the sea, "Peace! Be still!" And the wind ceased, and there was a great calm. He said to them, "Why are you so afraid? Have you still no faith?"*

They were absolutely with Jesus and Jesus was absolutely with them, but a storm came none-the-less. They were in the will of God and being obedient to go to the other side, yet a storm broke out that was treacherous and terrifying. But what did Jesus say to them? "Why are you so afraid?" We must refuse fear in any way, shape or form it comes. It must be a choice we make. We choose to believe God will make a way through this storm and there will be peace and calm where there had been turmoil and stress. Jesus gave them the very remedy for their fear – faith! He called for them to have faith. Fear drives out faith, but faith always drives out fear.

When our storm hit, we began doubting God's care for us and our dire situation. We became consumed with the thought that we weren't worthy for Him to help us. We had failed Him somehow and now He was rejecting our pleas for help. Just like the disciples in their storm who said to Jesus, "don't you care that we are perishing?" But our God ALWAYS cares! It is the enemy of our souls who brings condemnation and accusation against us. He will make you feel you are somehow disqualified from God's miracle power on your behalf. But His word is clear to us. Nahum 1:7 (ESV) *"The LORD is good, a stronghold in the day of trouble; He knows those who take refuge in Him."* When we seek His help and His divine intervention, just like He did for those disciples that day, He will rise up on our behalf because we have taken refuge in Him! Psalms 138:7 (ESV) "Though I walk in the midst of trouble, you preserve my life; you stretch out your hand against the wrath of my enemies, and your right hand delivers me."

Principle 2: *If you are praying, you will be led!*

If you are praying, God WILL show you whatever you need to do. He will lead you to the right place, the right people, or the right decision. Sometimes it takes more than one prayer, or one day of praying or one month! If we had stopped praying once we both had experienced God's peace that Saturday morning, Jim would never have received the next steps he was to take. He kept praying until he knew what God was now directing him to do. James 5:16-18b (ESV) *"The prayer of a righteous person has great power as it is working. Elijah was a man with a nature like ours, and he prayed fervently that it might not rain, and for three years and six months it did not rain on the earth. Then he prayed again, and heaven gave rain, and the earth bore its fruit."*

If we are praying to Jesus, turning to Him for guidance and direction, make no mistake about it – He is faithful to hear and answer. God answers PRAYER. The prayers Jim and I prayed mattered! Jim continuing to pray mattered. Because we were seeking Him and looking for His will, He was then able to speak to our hearts and reveal His will to us. During these times of praying,

God was setting things in motion. God was moving in our circumstances. Jim's friend was moved upon to call him up and check on him. The first man he was introduced to was moved upon not to hire him but instead introduce him to someone else. The third man was moved upon to make a decision to use Jim as the catalyst to fulfill his dream to build a restoration business. But it all started with the leading found in PRAYER!

Jesus has given us a wonderful promise that anchors our praying. John 10:4-5 (NLT2) *"After He has gathered His own flock, He walks ahead of them, and they follow him because they know His voice. They won't follow a stranger; they will run from him because they don't know his voice."* Jesus is letting us clearly know that if we are sincerely following Him, praying and seeking His guidance, and leading, we won't get it wrong. We won't follow the wrong voices because we know our Shepherd's voice. What a comfort. We can cast down all thoughts that we'll take the wrong path or make the wrong decision because it is Jesus who walks ahead of us, and we can just keep following.

Principle 3: *We have to let God do it His way.*

Jeremiah 18:2-4 (ESV) *"Arise, and go down to the potter's house, and there I will let you hear my words.' So I went down to the potter's house, and there he was working at his wheel. And the vessel he was making of clay was spoiled in the potter's hand, and he reworked it into another vessel, as it seemed good to the potter to do."*

Sometimes the things that fall apart in our lives are because God wants something different than we can see right now. Many times, we have to "let go" of how we want it to be in order to allow God to create what only He can create for us! Looking back to 1980 was such an eye-opener. Yes, Jim had a business. But it wasn't what he really loved or had a passion for. It was an income, a good business and successful but God knew Jim's heart and love - which was classic car restoration! God knew what would be more rewarding and fulfilling to Jim's life. But he had to let go of what he did have, in order for God to give him something better! I had to let go of my self-perceived security and what I thought it should look like, or the way it should happen, and find out that God is my security always – at all times.

If something becomes "*spoiled*" for you, take heart! Your Creator God has no limits. He creates out of nothing! And you will soon learn what Jim and I learned. *You don't need money. You just need God!*

PRAYER

Lord, I thank you that you are no respecter of persons. What you have done for one you will do for another. I relinquish my own ideas of how I think things must be. I give you my plans, my hopes, and my dreams. I give my problem into your capable hands, knowing you are forming me and my future on your potter's wheel and making something beautiful. Lead me in the way that I should go. Order my steps according to your plan. Your ways are perfect and right, and I know you are working all things together for my good and for your purpose. In Jesus name, Amen.

CHAPTER 11

The Art of Negotiations

Jaime Luce

It was after midnight. The house was still since everyone else had gone to bed. Joel sat in the quiet of the office with the doors closed ready to pray. Tonight, he was feeling the weight of the new mortgage and the addition of a new baby. Though it was all the abundant blessing of the Lord, it was also now more responsibility. He knew he was at the exact job that God had chosen for him, and in the house God had miraculously provided for our growing family. By all accounts we were doing very well.

He thought back to a prayer he'd prayed after rededicating his life to the Lord. He immediately had begun tithing on the little bit of money he had and told the Lord, "Even if I don't have enough money to pay my bills, I will give you the tithe first. And I know, someday, I'll be able to give you much more than this."

He had never made it a practice of asking the Lord for money specifically. He was more comfortable asking for the right connections or favor so that he could work and multiply what God had given him. Tonight, however, was different. He surprised himself when he heard his own spontaneous prayer. "God, if you will double my income, I will double my tithe." *That's a crazy prayer,* he thought. He didn't know if it was even biblical, but he prayed it nonetheless and felt God had accepted his prayer and believed He would do it.

Then, over the next several months, his business began to grow. As the year went on, the better and bigger things got. By the end of that year, God had done it. He doubled his income, but Joel had forgot to pay the double tithe. January went by. February went by. March went by. Then one night about 10:00 p.m., Joel was again sitting in the office and began to read his Bible. As he was reading, he came across a passage where the Lord was saying that it would have been better for you if you had never made an oath to me. And it hit him like a lightning bolt straight to his stomach, into his spirit, and deep into his soul. He physically crumbled and began to cry. The crying turned into bitter weeping. He said, "God I promised I would give you a double tithe. You did your part, but I didn't do mine." Joel cried until one o'clock in the morning. Through his tears he got up from the chair and went into the bedroom where I was asleep. He woke me up, and said, "Honey, I've got to tell you what I've done." He then told me everything that happened, what he said, what he prayed, and what he didn't do. I cried with him saying, "We have to give it."

The next day, Joel went and emptied out every account we had. Since that wasn't enough, we maxed our credit cards knowing this would really hurt. We would now also need to pay the interest, not just the payments. But he did it and pulled the money together. It took everything we had and could get our hands on. We expected that it would take quite some time to recover but it was our fault. We were just grateful that God was giving us the opportunity to get it right.

With the money now ready, we went to church that next Sunday and wrote the check out. It was a big check, an exceptionally large check. With a heavy repentant heart, he placed it in the envelope and dropped it in the offering. Under his breath he said, "Lord, now I know I've been obedient. You did what you said you were going to do. I didn't. Now I want to make it right."

That Wednesday, there was a business meeting at the church. The Pastor got up and began talking with a jubilant "Praise the Lord" and a "Hallelujah." "We're in the black," he said. "We were in the red until last Sunday." When he mentioned the amount that put us in the black, Joel knew God was talking to him directly. It was the exact amount of the check He'd given on Sunday.

God had accepted his offering. Then, within the next ninety days, God did the most merciful, and most undeserved act, by seeing to it that we got all that money back. Every single penny. Even though Joel hadn't done the right thing and delayed, God was merciful and accepted his offering, forgiving him on the spot. That would have been enough. But God not only accepted our offering and forgave us, He made it as if it had never happened. We were late by three months and within three months He had given it all back. What should have been a lengthy, costly, and justly deserved hardship and penalty, was reversed on our behalf.

This entire sequence of events only further displayed the heart of God toward us. He is not only our savior and provider but a redeemer and rewarder of obedience, even when we got it wrong before we got it right. If He says he will do it, He will do it. He knows what we have need of even before we ask. He hears the prayers we pray, and He honors His word. He is a covenant keeping God and He is good all the time, even when we don't deserve it.

In the end, no matter what you think you need, the answer is the same. *You don't need money. You just need God.* You'll never convince me otherwise.

PLAY CALL: *Let your "Yes" be yes and your "No" be no.*

Jesus said in Matthew 5:37, *"Just say a simple, 'Yes, I will,' or 'No, I won't.' Anything beyond this is from the evil one"*

(NLT). In other words, don't play games. Do what you say you're going to do. This single character trait has the power to bless or to curse. In the book of Judges, chapter eleven, we read the story of Jephthah. He had made a foolish vow to God for deliverance in battle, and it cost him his daughter. Proverbs 6:2 tells us that we can be trapped and ensnared by the words of our mouth. The night God spoke to Joel while reading his Bible, he read this. Ecclesiastes 5:4-8:

> *When you make a vow to God, do not be late in paying it; for He takes no delight in fools. Pay what you vow! It is better that you should not vow than that you should vow and not pay. Do not let your speech cause you to sin and do not say in the presence of the messenger of God that it was a mistake. Why should God be angry on account of your voice and destroy the work of your hands?* (NASB)

God never lies or makes empty promises. He is willing to bless us, but can God trust you with His blessing?

Every person who desires to be blessed will be tested. God will always do what He said He would do because He is a good father, and He is always trustworthy. But if you wish to be blessed you too will have to pass this test. When confronted with blessing, your character will determine whether you keep that blessing and favor or whether God allows it to be taken or destroyed.

LET YOUR "YES" BE YES AND YOUR "NO" BE NO
The Art of Negotiations

There are numerous scriptures that teach us to keep our vows, or in other words, keep our word. Deuteronomy 23:23 *"You shall be careful to perform what goes out from your lips, just as you have voluntarily vowed to the Lord your God, what you have promised"* (NASB).

Numbers 30:2 *"If a man makes a vow to the Lord, or takes an oath to bind himself with a binding obligation, he shall not violate his word; he shall do according to all that proceeds out of his mouth"* (NASB).

Matthew 5:33 *"Again, you have heard that the ancients were told, 'You shall not make false vows, but shall fulfill your vows to the Lord'"* (NASB).

These are just a few. This one lesson crosses into all areas of life. It affects everything. It is why it was such a vital lesson for Joel to learn. You might hear me say this over and over but that's because it's true. God wants to bless us. However, He will train and test our hearts to see if we will remain faithful, especially once we are blessed.

Principle 1: *God is concerned with the condition of your heart.*

Tithes and offerings, or in Joel's case an oath, are ways we come into covenant with the Lord over our finances. He requires adherence to His terms because He cares about the condition of your heart. His desire is always to bless us, but it is only a blessing when it draws us closer to Him instead of far from Him. Money and riches can be deceitful, so He gives specific instructions about handling money in order that our hearts remain pure and centered on Him, and that we aren't carried away by the love of money.

Money in and of itself is not evil. We've heard it misquoted, that money is the root of all evil. That is incorrect. The scripture actually says in 1 Timothy 6:10 (NIV) *"For the love of money is a root of all kinds of evil. Some people, eager for money, have wandered from the faith and pierced themselves with many griefs."* Whenever money is involved, the heart is involved. Your money will follow your heart. Matthew 6:21 (KJV) says, *"For where your treasure is, there will your heart be also."* God wanted to bless Joel and give him his request. But he also expected Joel to remain faithful and to guard his heart as he prospered him. *"For what shall it profit a man, if he shall gain the whole world, and lose his own soul?"* Mark 8:36 (KJV). Money isn't the problem. Our heart is.

Principle 2: *The Father's discipline is a show of his love and mercy.*

Hebrews 12:5-7 says,

> [5] *"And have you completely forgotten this word of encouragement that addresses you as a father addresses his son? It says, "My son, do not make light*

of the Lord's discipline, and do not lose heart when he rebukes you, ⁶ because the Lord disciplines the one he loves, and he chastens everyone he accepts as his son." ⁷ Endure hardship as discipline; God is treating you as his children. For what children are not disciplined by their father?" (NIV)

Joel could have taken what he read lightly. He could have thought that God was being too hard on him, expecting him to go into debt. The justification would sound something like, "God doesn't want us in debt. He wants us to be the lender and not the borrower." Or that after blessing him all year He surely wouldn't want him to have to empty every account and start over. He could have brushed off the stern correction he was reading by thinking that was just the Old Testament and now God gives grace. But God's grace was present, and His love was active. His mercy was to confront Joel and remind him of his oath. He was giving Joel an opportunity to make it right first before extending a correction or punishment. Had Joel rejected the loving correction of Father God, it would have been a completely different ending. But by humbling himself and repenting with true remorse, God did not withdraw the opportunity for blessing.

We see God's instruction to Moses in Deuteronomy 5:33 (NIV) *"Walk in obedience to all that the Lord your God has commanded you, so that you may live and prosper and prolong your days in the land that you will possess."* God's desire is to bless. That's why He teaches us His ways. One of which is that we will reap what we have sown. There is a reward for those who obey, a reaping, a blessing. But the opposite is also true. There is a consequence when we disobey. We will reap the bounty of our actions.

In 1 Kings chapter 15, God had Samuel the prophet, who anointed Saul as king, to tell him to go and destroy their enemy, the Amalekites. The instruction was to destroy everyone and everything and not to keep anything back. Saul began well by following the instructions and going to battle but when he saw the abundance of livestock, he decided that they were too valuable and could be useful to him. He didn't fully walk in the instruction he had received. He wasn't prepared to give all that he was required to give. In this decision, he disobeyed God's instructions. But partial obedience is disobedience. When Samuel confronted him about this, Saul tried to say that he planned on using the livestock as an offering to the Lord. He thought by sounding righteous or spiritual, that he could justify his disobedience. But God wasn't interested in the offering, or in today's vernacular, the money.

People love to justify their greed. They say things like, "God would want me to be blessed." Or "I'll give twice as much next time." We expect God to honor His word, but God also expects us to honor ours. To put it another way, God expects us to obey our own words and not make excuses.

> [22] So Samuel said: "Has the Lord as great delight in burnt offerings and sacrifices, as in obeying the voice of the Lord? Behold, to obey is better than sacrifice, and to heed than the fat of rams. [23] For rebellion is as the sin of witchcraft, and stubbornness is as iniquity and idolatry. Because you have rejected the word of the Lord, He also has rejected you from being king." [24] Then Saul said to Samuel, "I have sinned, for I have transgressed the commandment of the Lord and your words, because I feared the people and obeyed their voice. [25] Now therefore, please pardon my sin, and return with me, that I may worship the Lord." [26] But Samuel said to Saul, "I will not return with you, for you have rejected the word of the Lord, and the Lord has rejected you from being king over Israel." (NKJV)

By rejecting God's instructions, Saul was rejecting God himself. It is no different for us. Walking in blessing requires that we be trustworthy people.

Principle 3: *A broken oath is the same as lying to the Lord.*

The most shocking account is in the New Testament. It is that of Ananias and Sapphira who, like Saul, began well but who's end was tragic. They owned property and had promised to sell it and to give it to be dispersed to help provide for the needs of other Christian brother and sisters. That's a good thing. In fact, it's a very generous thing. The problem was that after they sold it, they agreed to lie about how much they sold it for to hold back a portion for themselves when that was never necessary. They could give freely whatever they desired to give and could have kept whatever they wanted to keep. Instead, they wanted the people to think they were giving all, and they lied to cover it up. It cost them everything.

> [1]*"Now a man named Ananias, together with his wife Sapphira, also sold a piece of property.* [2] *With his wife's full knowledge he kept back part of the money for himself but brought the rest and put it at the apostles' feet.* [3] *Then Peter said, "Ananias, how is it that Satan has so filled your heart that you have lied to the Holy Spirit and have kept for yourself some of the money you received for the land?* [4]*Didn't it belong to you before it was sold? And after it was sold, wasn't the money at your disposal? What made you think of doing such a thing? You have not lied just to human beings but to God." * [5] *When Ananias heard this, he fell down and died. And great fear seized all who heard what had happened.* [6]*Then some young*

men came forward, wrapped up his body, and carried him out and buried him. ⁷About three hours later his wife came in, not knowing what had happened. ⁸Peter asked her, "Tell me, is this the price you and Ananias got for the land?" "Yes," she said, "that is the price." ⁹Peter said to her, "How could you conspire to test the Spirit of the Lord? Listen! The feet of the men who buried your husband are at the door, and they will carry you out also." ¹⁰At that moment she fell down at his feet and died. Then the young men came in and, finding her dead, carried her out and buried her beside her husband.

(Acts 5:1-10, NIV)

The Lord takes our promises seriously. Just as we expect God to keep His promises, He expects the same of us. If you feel that God did not keep a promise to you, you must look inward. Is there any place of disobedience? Was there a place where he instructed you, but you chose another way? If that is the case, you must humble yourself. Psalms 51 tells us that God won't despise a broken and contrite spirit. He promises that if we humble ourselves, He will lift us up. A fallen condition does not need to be permanent. Simply start today. Just make it right.

To want to be blessed isn't evil. Ecclesiastes even goes so far as to say that money answers all things. It isn't wrong to desire more money. God wants to bless you. His desire is that you live a life full of goodness and plenty. But we must always be on guard.

Joel wanted God more than he wanted the money. He really did want to honor his promise. With the busyness of work and the success of the business Joel forgot about his promise. God did not. And it was His mercy that He didn't. God's correction was certainly his love for us, and it is for you too.

So go ahead and ask. He's ready to answer and He desires to bless you. Remember, He's a good Father. And if you'll let Him, He'll show you that *you don't need money. You just need God.*

PRAYER

Lord, there is none as good as you. You are righteous in all that you do. You teach me your ways so that I might know you, so that I might be blessed. Thank you for wanting to keep me close to your heart, and always offering me a way back to you when I've drifted far from you. If I have made excuses, please show them to me and where my heart has faltered. I want to know truth and I ask for your forgiveness. If I have not kept my vow, show me the way back to your heart. I desire you and I want to be blessed by you. Thank you for your mercy, for hearing my prayer, and for blessing me. In Jesus's name, Amen.

CHAPTER 12

Death and Taxes

Jaime Luce

With the large double doors closed, I sat in the quiet of our home office when my phone rang, breaking the silence. My husband Joel was calling from work. I could hear the stress in his voice as he began to tell me what he'd just learned. I was almost used to hearing bad news at this point. The housing crash of 2008 had set in motion an excruciating couple of years. We watched as the news continued to tell gut wrenching stories of so many losing their homes and businesses. Most commercial print business were forced to close their doors affecting people we knew personally. By God's grace we were still in business, but there were many days when we didn't know if the doors would close that night for good.

On that phone call Joel began to tell me that we now owed the IRS $300,000.00. I'm glad he couldn't see my face. I know my panicked glossy-eyed stare would have made it so much worse and only added to the pressure he was carrying. I was grateful to be on the phone. How could we owe that much? The business had lost so much money. We had already been forced to restructure. Every possible way was already in motion to keep the plates spinning. It just didn't seem possible. We didn't have the money to pay that bill.

My fear was fueled by having watched too many movies of the IRS confiscating everything. We weren't criminals, of course, but I let all those crazy stories run through my mind. I thought about Leona Helmsley's two hundred and fifty pairs of famously auctioned shoes and tax evasion arrest. I even thought about Bernie Madoff and his outrageous Ponzi schemes. How could this be real? I entertained that little melt down in my mind for days.

Then one morning something happened. Joel went into the bathroom to get ready for work. I suddenly felt an urgency to go to our praying chair. It was a cream cushioned glider and footstool we kept in the corner of our home office. After years of rocking kids to bed and saying bedtime prayers, it had become our favorite place to pray. I grabbed my Bible from off the side table as I looked out the big picture window. It was a cloudy morning. The sky was dark and grey, and the clouds were low and heavy. It strangely felt warm like a blanket. It felt so good that I didn't turn the lights on. I quickly realized what I was feeling was the presence of the Lord that had just come into the room. I was ready to talk to Him and He with me. It was as if He was anticipating the look on my face when I read His words to me that day.

My custom of reading is to just pick up where I left off. I don't follow a reading plan. I start at the beginning and continue to the end. That morning the Lord knew where I had left off. He knew where I was, and He was about to share something with me. I'm convinced that the urgency I felt that morning was His excitement. He couldn't wait to show me what He was going to do. As I opened my Bible my eyes fixed on the text, *"having canceled the charge of our legal indebtedness, which stood against us and condemned us; he has taken it away, nailing it to the cross"* Colossians 2:14 (NIV).

I don't think I can adequately put into words what I felt at that moment. He literally just told me that the "legal charge" that we were indebted to pay, which stood against us, condemning us, has been revoked! He paid it all already! The work he had done on the cross was not just for the removal of my sin, but also the provision of all I would ever need.

I immediately felt strength surge through me. An excitement filled me that I struggled to contain. My God had just told me that He had taken care of it. I knew that was His voice, and it was a done deal! You couldn't convince me otherwise. He answered me like He had so many other times before. I didn't have to worry about that anymore. I didn't know how He would do it and I didn't care! I just knew it was done.

I jumped out of that chair and ran straight to the shower with happy tears streaming down my face to tell Joel what God had just told me. I was talking so fast and with such a squeal that he couldn't understand a word I was saying. He told me to slow down and tell him again. I slowed myself down and explained what had just happened and what the scripture said. I told him I know in the depths of my spirit that God had fixed it.

Now you must understand. Joel is the one who has to deal with all this. He is the one who has to "fix" it or "find the solution." He is the business owner. He is the responsible party, the head of our house. God had told this to me in grand fashion, but Joel is simply hearing it from me. I tried to assure him that God would show him how or what, but that God had done it.

The following week, Joel had a scheduled meeting with our CPA to discuss the taxes. And just like deja vu, it happened again. I was in the office sitting in my praying chair when my phone rang. Joel was leaving the tax accountant and couldn't wait to call me. He told me how that while they were discussing everything, the tax accountant suddenly remembered a new tax law. He explained that due to the recession and businesses struggling to remain open, they were offering what is called a loss carry back. Essentially that means that you are able to take the losses that you have incurred from previous years and apply it toward this year's taxes. He told Joel they would re-run the numbers. When he did, it changed everything! Joel said, "Not only do we not owe $300,000.00, but we are getting back $380,000.00! I started screaming. I knew it! God did it! Praise God! I quoted Romans 10:11 (NASB) which says, *"Whoever believes in Him will never be put to shame."* I was beside myself with joy. We wouldn't lose our home. We wouldn't close the business doors today and I wouldn't have my shoes carried off by the IRS.

Now I know that the scripture God shared with me that morning in context is about our sins. I don't argue that. What I find fascinating is that God is so big and so wonderful that He can speak to me in every moment and in every circumstance right out of His Word to tell me something very specific. Had I read that verse in a different translation that morning, I wouldn't have received the exact words I needed to hear that day. God is in the details.

I know that the expectation I felt along with the very real presence of God was because He is exactly what He says He is. He is an ever-present help in the time of trouble. He is so personal that He knows what translation of the Bible I'm reading. He knows how to speak to me so that I will hear Him. And He knows how to talk to you too. He can prepare the moment for you just like

He did for me. Every question I have, He has the answer. He has proved over and over again that *you don't need money. You just need God*. And if you'll give Him the chance, He will prove it to you too.

PLAY CALL: *Know Your Benefits.*

The Bible is comprised of the Old and New Testament which contains instructions for living a victorious life in Jesus. In a matter of speaking, it is Jesus's Will and Testament left for us. Someone who passes away, leaving a will, leaves instructions for what is to be done with and to whom their possessions and assets are to be left. The instructions may be very specific in how something is to be given or used in order for a person to receive. It is at the reading of the will that you find out what is left to you and how you are to receive it. Without the reading, no one would know if they were mentioned and subsequently if anything was left to them.

As a believer in Jesus Christ, you have been named in His will. He has a plan and a purpose for your life. He has prepared and reserved all the provision you will need as you follow His instructions spelled out in His Will. They are all available to you if you will simply read the Will. I have good news. You've not been left out. You are a benefactor of His will. What you need has not been left to another. He has set in motion plans to bless you and to provide for you for the rest of your life. To find out what He's left to you simply schedule a reading. This is exactly what I did that day in my office. I knew the Lord was calling me to a reading. He wanted to show me what He had left me. And He wants to show you what He's left you.

IT PAYS TO KNOW YOUR BENEFITS
Death and Taxes

Merriam-Webster defines a benefit as something that produces good or helpful results, a useful aid, financial help, a payment or service provided, or a service or right provided by an employer. When used as a verb it means, useful for profitability and to receive help or an advantage. King David told us in Psalms 103:2, *"Bless the Lord, O my Soul, and forget not all his benefits"* (KJV). He then goes on to list twenty verses containing a host of those benefits. Just take a minute to think about that. King David instructs us to *not forget* "all" the benefits afforded to us by God. So according to the Merriam-Webster, serving the Lord provides good and helpful results. He provides useful aid and financial help. He provides payment and services, and I am afforded rights under His plan for my life. He then makes my situation useful for my profitability and gives me an advantage. Wow! That is exactly what God did for us. He in essence, took what the devil meant for evil and made it good and profitable for us. Instead of owing a bill we received a check. The same word benefit in the *Strong's Concordance* means accomplishment and requital. Because of the cross, I receive the benefits that He deserved and not that I deserved. To not receive them or make use of them is to lessen the value I put on His sacrifice. *He paid too high a price for us not to remember and make use of the benefits He purchased for us.*

Principle 1: *Schedule a reading.*

Benefits come in all shapes and sizes. A smart job applicant will want to know what the salary and benefits are before accepting a job. Some jobs may not pay a large salary but provide wonderful benefits. With things like a great health insurance plan or lengthy paid vacation time, an applicant may feel it's worth it to take the job. You could have a senior management position that pays severance even after you leave a job. Some employers pay for continuing education for their employees or provide you with a car.

Jeremiah 29:11 tells us *"For I know the plans I have for you, declares the Lord, "plans to prosper you and not to harm you, plans to give you a hope and a future"* (NIV). If you knew what God had planned for you, you'd want it. But here is the caveat with wills. You have to claim what it is that is left to you. I could open a bank account and put a million dollars in it with your name on it. If you don't know it's there, how will you ever benefit from it? He

YOU DON'T NEED MONEY, YOU JUST NEED GOD

will not force His will on you. You must choose His will. You must choose to read His instructions and choose to receive all He has prepared for you. It really is up to you.

In our tax situation, had we not known about the benefit of a tax law we could have had an entirely different outcome with life altering consequences. Taking our problem to someone who knows the benefits afforded us a solution to our problem. In fact, instead of a problem we were left a blessing. Joel 2:14 *"Who knows? Perhaps he will give you a reprieve, sending you a blessing instead of this curse. Perhaps you will be able to offer grain and wine to the LORD your God as before."* (NLT) Knowing the benefits can turn it all around for you just as it did for us.

Principle 2: *Don't squander your inheritance.*

Google's definition of squander is to waste (something, especially money or time) in a reckless and foolish manner. To allow (an opportunity) to pass or be lost.

The most classic example of this is found in Luke 15:11-32 (ESV):

> *[11] And he said, "There was a man who had two sons. [12] And the younger of them said to his father, 'Father, give me the share of property that is coming to me.' And he divided his property between them. [13] Not many days later, the younger son gathered all*

he had and took a journey into a far country, and there he squandered his property in reckless living. [14] And when he had spent everything, a severe famine arose in that country, and he began to be in need. [15] So he went and hired himself out to one of the citizens of that country, who sent him into his fields to feed pigs. [16] And he was longing to be fed with the pods that the pigs ate, and no one gave him anything.

[17] "But when he came to himself, he said, 'How many of my father's hired servants have more than enough bread, but I perish here with hunger! [18] I will arise and go to my father, and I will say to him, "Father, I have sinned against heaven and before you. [19] I am no longer worthy to be called your son. Treat me as one of your hired servants.'" [20] And he arose and came to his father. But while he was still a long way off, his father saw him and felt compassion, and ran and embraced him and kissed him. [21] And the son said to him, 'Father, I have sinned against heaven and before you. I am no longer worthy to be called your son.' [22] But the father said to his servants, 'Bring quickly the best robe, and put it on him, and put a ring on his hand, and shoes on his feet. [23] And bring the fattened calf and kill it and let us eat and celebrate. [24] For this my son was dead, and is alive again; he was lost, and is found.' And they began to celebrate.

The prodigal son had every opportunity afforded him by his father. He knew the father's will yet chose to leave it. He thought he could do it on his own and for a while it seemed to work. He squandered all of his living. *He went from having it all to having nothing at all.* The beauty of this story is that though he wasted it all, his father never changed his plan or his will for his son.

If this is you, it's time to go home to your Father. It's not too late, and He hasn't changed His mind. You may have tried it on your own. You may have demanded your way. But today I'm here to tell you, you are not disqualified. It doesn't matter what your past holds. Even if you were in the Father's house before and left. Even if you squandered all He had given you. You can return and receive the best of the benefits. He's looking for you and longing for your return. He wants to restore you and provide for your needs. He isn't angry. He loves you and cares about the pain that drove you to the pig pen. He's telling you today to come home. Don't spend another day eating slop. Your Father has prepared your robe, your ring, and the food for a celebration like no other. Don't squander the opportunity for redemption. Choose today to receive your inheritance.

If, however, this isn't you and you've remained in the Father's house, it is still possible that you have squandered your inheritance. Let's look now at the older brother:

²⁵ "Now his older son was in the field, and as he came and drew near to the house, he heard music and dancing. ²⁶ And he called one of the servants and asked what these things meant. ²⁷ And he said to him, 'Your brother has come, and your father has killed the fattened calf, because he has received him back safe and sound.' ²⁸ But he was angry and refused to go in. His father came out and entreated him, ²⁹ but he answered his father, 'Look, these many years I have served you, and I never disobeyed your command, yet you never gave me a young goat, that I might celebrate with my friends. ³⁰ But when this son of yours came, who has devoured your property with prostitutes, you killed the fattened calf for him!' ³¹ And he said to him, 'Son, you are always with me, and all that is mine is yours. ³² It was fitting to celebrate and be glad, for this your brother was dead, and is alive; he was lost, and is found.'" (ESV)

Let's look again at the second Google definition: To allow (an opportunity) to pass or be lost. The older brother was jealous of the blessing that the younger had received. He felt that he was undeserving and pious that he had not wasted anything. But his anger was misplaced. Look at what the Father says to him. '*Son, you are always with me, and all that is mine is yours.*'

It didn't matter what was given to his younger brother. All that the father has belongs to him. The father never stopped the eldest brother from celebrating or taking advantage of the benefits of being his father's son. He never took the opportunity afforded him. Instead, he squandered it.

As a Christian, Christ has paid the full price for your salvation. The purchase price He paid includes many benefits. What a tragedy it would be to walk out this Christian life, not knowing or making use of all the benefits allotted to you. It would be like having that million-dollar inheritance left to you, but you never bothered to go to the reading of the will. What could you be missing out on right now? What provision has already been made for you that you haven't taken hold of? Don't waste any more time. Don't squander another opportunity. Read the will and claim your benefits. Joel 2:14 *Who knows? Perhaps he will give you a reprieve, sending you a blessing instead of this curse. Perhaps you will be able to offer grain and wine to the LORD your God as before.* (NLT) He did it for me and He will do it for you. Let's pray.

PRAYER

Father I am so grateful for the sacrifice that you have paid for me. Thank you for making all your provisions and benefits available to me. I don't want to squander another day or opportunity that you have afforded me. Though I have done nothing to deserve them you still desire to give them to me. Today, I choose your will. I desire for you to speak to me through your Word and lead me into your provision and plan. I know your plans for me are good and I am so blessed to be called your child. I receive all you have for me today. In Jesus's name, Amen.

CHAPTER 13

When Little is Much

Jaime Luce

What began with my grandmother was passed to my parents, then passed to us, their children. My siblings and I are now endeavoring to pass this powerful legacy to our children and our grandchildren. This chapter is to encourage you that no matter your age, God's principles work. Our children can know God's power now and not waste time or money learning to trust and obey God's instructions for blessing and provision. The earlier they learn it, the better. Scripture teaches that we are to *"Train up a child in the way he should go. And when he is old, he will not depart from it."* Proverbs 22:6 (KJV). This is the story of my sister Jenny's daughter.

While serving on the audio/visual team in the sound booth at the back of the sanctuary, McKenzie sat in the dark with an elevated view of the room. She was taking notes while listening to the Australian guest minister who was speaking to her church youth group. The presence of the Lord was tangible, and she could feel the nudging of the Holy Spirt as He prodded her to pay attention to what was being said. The minister was speaking about giving in faith. Not usually a topic that a minister would speak about when addressing a youth group.

McKenzie grew curious as he began to tell the story of his youth group back in Australia. After a message much like the one he was preaching now, his youth group, which consisted of a hundred and fifty young people, gave sacrificially by faith into the offering. That night his youth group gave an astounding $15,000 to support the needs of that same group. McKenzie was blown away. She'd never heard of a youth group, who usually don't have much money, giving such an incredibly large offering. The story gripped her because she had a very real and present need herself. She also didn't have much money. *Where would the offering come from? What was God saying?*, she thought.

McKenzie was an extremely hard working, dedicated, junior in High School. Her care for her education was evidenced by AP classes, a Varsity spot on the Polo team, and a 4.25 grade point average. Her end goal for school was a degree in the medical field. And as a Junior, she had her eyes set on college. While her parents were beyond proud of her, they had no current means to send her to college, let alone cover a medical degree. And based off her two older siblings' experiences, and knowing her parent's income had not changed much, she wouldn't qualify for help from government loans. But McKenzie wasn't giving up. Though she is quiet by nature and happy to remain in the background, she has tremendous strength, fortitude, and tenacity. She wanted to go to school which to her obviously meant God would need to intervene. She began by asking God in prayer for the tuition. She didn't know the process of where to begin or how to go about it. All she knew was to put her trust in the Lord. She believed He would show her what school to attend, and then how to pay for it.

She sat quietly listening to the rest of the message. He taught them about sowing by the leading of the Spirit and believing in faith. Which is to say that we sow when we hear the voice and direction of the Spirit of God and believe that what we need we've received by faith, because we have sown the seed that will produce the harvest we need.

McKenzie felt something she'd never felt before. She knew it was the Holy Spirit stirring inside her heart. He told her, in an almost audible voice, "Give it. Put your faith to the test. Sow your money and give to your youth group." It almost startled her. She was a full-time student with AP classes, who also played athletics. What she had was a little birthday money she'd saved and the money she'd earned working for a few weeks during the summer. The grand total was about $300. It was just enough to buy her annual Disneyland pass to use with friends which they were all preparing to do. Was God really asking her to give that up? As she thought about it and what she knew about God, she realized, "God wouldn't ask me to give away the one thing I want for no reason." She understood that He was telling her to give her offering in faith. Sow it, and He would provide her school tuition.

Though the room was full of people, there in the dark of the sound booth, it was just Jesus and McKenzie. This was her defining moment. Up to this point, she'd never been confronted by a decision like this. Financial needs were handled by her parents. Her personal faith and walk with God had not yet been tested. She had not been faced with this kind of self-sacrifice before. If she obeyed what she felt the Lord was asking her to do, it would mean that she could not do what she'd prepared to do. Giving up her hard-earned Disney pass was a difficult decision and one that would hurt. She admittedly was torn because she knew without a job, she wouldn't be able to gain that money back. So even though she'd heard the Lord's direction, she also felt the sorrow of losing what she'd worked for. She had to make a choice.

So, with an obedient heart, McKenzie gave. She obeyed the direction of the Holy Spirit. She knew it would mean not getting a Disney pass and missing out on the many times her friends would go without her. Even though sadness came with her obedience, she knew that you don't trust emotions. You trust God. And when you do, He is faithful.

For the next couple of months, McKenzie watched as her friends enjoyed their Disney passes over and over and all without her. She could have begun to get angry or remorseful and allow doubt to creep in. Instead, her attitude remained one of expectation. It didn't shake her. She remained in faith that God was providing an answer, and that He would honor her sacrifice.

Then came the moment of truth. It was time to turn in college applications. The school she felt directed to apply to was California Baptist University, a private institution. Because it was private, the tuition costs were more than average. But McKenzie was walking by faith. It doesn't matter what the amount is when you don't have any money anyway. Right?

McKenzie began filing for scholarships and grants, hoping to gain some help with tuition. It wasn't long before a letter addressed to McKenzie from CBU arrived. There it was in black and white, but to no one's surprise, McKenzie's acceptance letter. As soon as she read it, she immediately went online to check her financial aid statement for the status of the scholarships and grant offers. To her amazement as she scrolled through the list, she had garnered and qualified for over $32,000, and she would receive that amount of money every year for the next four years. It was more than she needed. God turned her $300 offering into $120,000. God had just proved to McKenzie, that *You don't need money. You just need God!*

And because our God is so good and so personal, McKenzie received a phone call from someone she had gone to kindergarten with. They were coming into town and wanted to take her to Disneyland! McKenzie was so excited. Her friend not only bought the Disney ticket but bought the hopper pass allowing them to go back and forth between the Disney and California Adventure parks.

Then, immediately upon graduation, McKenzie was hired for the very job she wanted. She quickly saved enough money to buy her own annual pass and began going with friends. She could enjoy it so much more now.

You might think that this is the end of the story. But God wasn't finished. McKenzie continued to earn more scholarships through her job and from other places. The blessings just kept coming. When it was all said and done, the total came out to approximately $140,000 which not only covered the tuition that subsequently increased as the years continued, but it also covered all other school expenses she encountered.

McKenzie said, "I never would have dreamed that I would be able to go to college virtually free. I have never forgotten the importance of the lesson God taught me that night. I had to be patient as I watched my friends go to my favorite place without me. But in the end, I got both my school covered and I got to go with my friends." She knew it was the grace of God that she heard and obeyed the Lord that Wednesday night. Studious as she is, she passed her faith test with flying colors, reminding us again, that we don't need money. We just need God.

PLAY CALL: *Sow by the leading of the Spirit in faith.*

The practice of giving in faith is used secularly every day. When you pay in advance for any kind of service, you are believing you will get something in return that is worth the prepayment you have made. If, for instance, you need to have a surgery, you are expected to pay your co-pay before the surgery takes place. The doctor doesn't say, "let me know if you're happy with the outcome and then feel free to pay me what you think it's worth." Like McKenzie, if you want to attend school, you must pay a tuition. You are believing you will receive an education and degree that is worthy of the money you have paid. They don't say, "Come and learn, and if you think you've received a good education you can tip your professors."

Neither does God operate as a waiter or waitress. He doesn't take your order and then ask for tips if you are satisfied with how what you ordered turned out. If you can understand this concept, you can understand sowing in faith. In fact, your confidence in your return should be even greater when sowing into the creators' hands. He is the "I am." Whatever you need, He is. If He's the one who told you to give, sowing by the Spirit is your insurance policy on your investment. It's just like insider trading. The Spirit of God is telling you something before it even happens. And God already has a plan in place to give you the return on your investment if you'll just follow His direction.

SOW BY THE LEADING OF THE SPIRIT IN FAITH
When Little is Much

There will be times when God asks you to let go of what you have, to give you what you don't have. Only those who are willing to trust the Lord will receive what can only be obtained by faith. What is faith? "Now faith is the substance of things hoped for and the evidence of things not seen" Romans 11:1 (KJV). It's a substantive trust that says you will have what you've hoped for now, even though there is no evidence yet. A great example in scripture is that of Elijah and the widow at Zarephath in 1 Kings 17:7-15 (NKJV):

> [8] *Then the word of the Lord came to him, saying,* [9] *"Arise, go to Zarephath, which belongs to Sidon,*

and dwell there. See, I have commanded a widow there to provide for you." ¹⁰ So he arose and went to Zarephath. And when he came to the gate of the city, indeed a widow was there gathering sticks. And he called to her and said, "Please bring me a little water in a cup, that I may drink." ¹¹ And as she was going to get it, he called to her and said, "Please bring me a morsel of bread in your hand." ¹² So she said, "As the Lord your God lives, I do not have bread, only a handful of flour in a bin, and a little oil in a jar; and see, I am gathering a couple of sticks that I may go in and prepare it for myself and my son, that we may eat it, and die." ¹³ And Elijah said to her, "Do not fear; go and do as you have said, but make me a small cake from it first, and bring it to me; and afterward make some for yourself and your son. ¹⁴ For thus says the Lord God of Israel: 'The bin of flour shall not be used up, nor shall the jar of oil run dry, until the day the Lord sends rain on the earth.'" ¹⁵ So she went away and did according to the word of Elijah; and she and he and her household ate for many days. ¹⁶ The bin of flour was not used up, nor did the jar of oil run dry, according to the word of the Lord which He spoke by Elijah.

This passage says that God had commanded a widow "there" to provide. This sounds so similar to the miracle of Jesus feeding the 5,000. John 6:6 (NLT) says *"He was testing Philip, for he already knew what he was going to do."* God was already working a miracle before Elijah ever made it to the widow's house. So, following the Lord's instructions is paramount. The word of the Lord is the principal thing. It was the word that Elijah heard, delivered, and that manifested the harvest. The word is delivered by the Spirit of God because the Spirit of God is in unity with the heart of God. Those who learn to listen to Him and act on His word will see the manifestation of it.

Elijah, the prophet, lived by the word of God. His job as a prophet was to hear and deliver God's message. The word of God carries the power of God to perform the word. Isaiah 55:11 (ESV) says *"so shall my word be that goes out from my mouth; it shall not return to me empty, but it shall accomplish that which I purpose, and shall succeed in the thing for which I sent it."* When you have the word, an instruction, or promise from the Lord by His Spirit, you are guaranteed that it will come to pass. Because of this guarantee we are told not to fear.

Elijah was given a directive from the Lord to go to a particular widow in a particular place because the Lord had commanded a widow there to feed him. When Elijah gets there, the widow is out collecting sticks to literally cook her last meal. Elijah, because He was told by the Lord, tells her to feed him first and then promises that if she does, her oil and meal will not run out. In this exchange are the principles for sowing by the Spirit in faith.

Principle 1: *The Spirit initiates the offering.*

God spoke to Elijah. Because Elijah knew what God was planning to do, he boldly made the request to feed him first with the last of her supply, and then told her not to fear. If she was willing, He promised that God would do a miracle and her food would not run out. The Lord would sustain her until the famine was over.

Just as Elijah brought the word of God to the widow, the Holy Spirit brings the word to us. He knows what God is planning to do and gives us the instruction so that we can access it by faith. McKenzie heard the Holy Spirit tell her to give it and He'd provide. For both the widow and for McKenzie, it hurt to give what they had, but God gives us a wonderful promise when we give what is precious to us. Psalms 126:5 (KJ21) says, *"He that goeth forth and weepeth, bearing precious seed, shall doubtless come again with rejoicing, bringing his sheaves with him."* We may weep but not for long. In Psalms 30:5 (NKJV) we're promised that *"Weeping may endure for a night, but joy comes in the morning."*

God says, if you'll trust Him with your seed, especially when it's such a sacrifice, you can be sure He will turn your tears into laughter and rejoicing when your harvest comes in. He knows it's precious to you which is why it's such valuable and potent seed. I've said it before, and I'll say it again. If you knew what God had for you, you'd want it.

1 Corinthians 2:9-16 says:

> [9] *"But as it is written, eye has not seen, nor ear heard, nor have entered into the heart of man, the things which God has prepared for them that love him.* [10]*But God has revealed them unto us by his Spirit: for the Spirit searches all things, yes, the deep things of God.* [11] *For what man knows the things of a man except the spirit of the man which is in him? Even so no one knows the things of God except the Spirit of God.* [12] *Now we have received, not the spirit of the world, but the Spirit who is from God, that we might know the things that have been freely given to us by God."* (NKJV)

God has the answer to your need. He wants to meet that need to the point that you no longer have a need. In fact, He wants to give you more than enough. Ephesians 3:20 says, "Now to Him who is able to do exceedingly abundantly above all that we ask or think, according to the power that works in us" (NKJV).

Principal 2: *The ground you sow into matters.*

God told Elijah to go to a specific land and to a specific person. He will do the same with you. That's because God has already determined and commanded a blessing for you there. It is a place He has already prepared. Just as God first created the garden of Eden and then placed Adam in it, so God will go ahead of you and prepare the place that is already blessed for you.

The scriptures are riddled with this principle. 2 Kings five talks about Naaman the leper. The prophet told him to go to the Jordan river and dip seven times and he'd be healed. He almost went away without a healing because he wanted to go to a different river or at least a cleaner river. He thought he knew better. It was the wise council of his servant that convinced him to obey. That one decision to go where he was commanded saved his life.

If Elijah had gone to an adjacent town looking for a widow, there would have been no miracle. God's instructions are like street-by-street directions on a map that is designed to get you to a particular destination. They are exact so that you arrive at the right place at the right time, to receive the right outcome. Making a right when he says left will mean you'll miss your mark. God's word is an invitation to receive the gifts and blessing He has planned for you. But you must go where He has made preparation.

The widow sowed into Elijah because she believed the Word of the Lord through him. She knew that her need would go unmet unless God intervened. By faith she obeyed even in her dire condition and because she obeyed, she, her son, and the prophet, ate well through the entire drought.

McKenzie sowed $300. It was all she had. She, like the widow, already had plans for that. The widow expected to use what she had to eat her last meal. McKenzie had intended to plant that seed into Disneyland's soil, expecting a harvest of fun with friends. Had the widow ignored the word of the Lord, she would have eaten but she also would have ultimately starved. Had McKenzie ignored the Spirit of the Lord, she would have gone to Disneyland, but she ultimately wouldn't have gone to college. Because the widow gave to Elisha, they ate that meal and every other meal. Because McKenzie gave her gift to her youth group, the youth group was cared for, and she got to go to college for free, as well as go to Disneyland.

Jesus lets us know that the outcome will be determined by the ground. That's why He declares the "where." Matthew 13:3-9 (NKJV):

> [3] *Then He spoke many things to them in parables, saying: "Behold, a sower went out to sow. [4] And as he sowed, some seed fell by the wayside; and the birds came and devoured them. [5] Some fell on stony places, where they did not have much earth; and*

> *they immediately sprang up because they had no*
> *depth of earth.* *⁶ But when the sun was up they were*
> *scorched, and because they had no root they with-*
> *ered away.* *⁷ And some fell among thorns, and the*
> *thorns sprang up and choked them.* *⁸ But others fell*
> *on good ground and yielded a crop: some a hun-*
> *dredfold, some sixty, some thirty.* *⁹ He who has ears*
> *to hear, let him hear!"*

Ground that is considered good soil means that the soil has been prepared to receive seed. And the harvest that comes from it will be determined by the condition of that ground. It is therefore imperative to follow the leading of the Holy Spirit when sowing. You may receive a harvest sowing the ground you choose, but your harvest, if it comes, will be short lived and lacking what you really need. Had McKenzie sown the seed to Disneyland, she would have received the harvest she thought she wanted but she would not have received the harvest she needed, nor what God had prepared for her. God's harvest is always far greater.

Principal 3: *Stay in faith as you wait.*

Do you realize that every day the widow had to go to the same flour and oil, and every day it was enough? She had to remain in faith. McKenzie watched for months, as her friends were going and enjoying their passes without her. In Genesis 8:22, God is explaining his promise to Noah after he exited the ark. He tells him that as long as the earth remains, there will be seed time and harvest. God is saying that you can trust me. This you can count on.

What always strikes me about that passage is seed time. There is always going to be a time to sow. Sowing however is always in faith. When you plant a crop, you don't know how it will turn out until after the cold of winter or the heat of summer. To me, that is the time. Seed time of course is a time to plant seed. But the not so obvious fact is that after the seed comes time. You can't make it grow any faster. You can't take it early. It takes what it takes. Time is necessary for a good harvest. Remaining in faith during that time also affects your harvest.

1 Peter 1:7 (NLT) tells us *"⁷ These trials will show that your faith is genuine. It is being tested as fire tests and purifies gold—though your faith is far more precious than mere gold. So when your faith remains strong through many trials, it will bring you much praise and glory and honor on the day when Jesus Christ is revealed to the whole world."* Your faith will always be tried. James 1:2-4 (NIV) puts it this way, *²Consider it pure joy, my brothers and sisters, whenever you face trials of many kinds, ³ because you know that the testing of your faith produces perseverance. ⁴ Let perseverance finish its work so that you may be mature and complete, not*

lacking anything. Both the widow and McKenzie lacked nothing. They received by faith everything they needed. God had spoken to McKenzie's heart and said, "Put your faith to the test." He was wanting to show McKenzie she could always trust Him to meet her needs. He's faithful and always will be. Philippians 1:6 (AMP) *"I am convinced and confident of this very thing, that He who has begun a good work in you will (continue to) perfect and complete it util the day of Christ Jesus. (The time of His return)"*

We don't have to fear the time. With God, time is on our side. You won't run out too early. God will see to it that you have what you need, when you need it, and for how long you need it. He's trustworthy. So, stay in faith. Keep your joy and allow your confidence to grow. The testing of your faith will in the end produce a harvest. Your joy will be complete.

Don't hesitate to obey. Sowing by the leading of the Spirit in faith is God's way to a sure harvest.

PRAYER

Father, I bow my heart before you in quiet trust. I know you are my provider. You will not withhold any good thing from me. Show me if You want me to sow for my harvest. I can trust that You will bring about a bountiful supply and meet my need completely if I obey. Show me the ground that I am to sow into, so I don't waste and squander my seed. And help me to remain in faith, knowing the Holy Spirit is my guarantee that what You've said, you will do. For this I give You praise. In Jesus's name, Amen.

CHAPTER 14

It's All or Nothing

Jaime Luce

It was Christmas Eve, and I was about eight or nine years old. My siblings and I were watching television in Grandma's den. At midnight I had run out of patience. I kept moving back and forth between the couch and the chair inwardly having a fit. I wanted to open the gifts and celebrate Christmas. I was getting tired, and my throat was beginning to hurt from the lump I was putting there out of angst. But by the sound of the prayer meeting happening in the other room, I knew we were still going to have to wait.

Many years later, our Christmas Eves look much the same. Grandma had begun a special tradition that would endure no matter how bad we wanted to open those gifts. It was on one such Christmas Eve that my husband Joel was in the *"Hot Seat."* This is what we called the seat that sat in the center of the room. Each person would find themselves in that chair at some point in the night. Everyone gathered around, with their hands lain on you, and they all prayed for you. Some might say it's the hot seat because by the time we were done praying for you, you were hot from all of us gathered around you and those praying were sweating from praying so hard. But Mom would say it was because it's where the Holy Fire would fall. Regardless of why, we've seen some wonderful miracles come from that special time.

To begin the *"Hot Seat"* prayer, the person in the chair would tell us what they were asking and believing God for. I guess you could say it was a sort of Christmas gift request. Many times, it was something we needed a real breakthrough in, or just things we'd like to see God do, change, or give direction on. It was my husband Joel's turn. This time he had a different request.

He had been wrestling with what he felt God had dropped into his spirit. Up to this time, Joel was now a very successful salesperson. God had truly blessed and multiplied him at the company God led him too several years earlier. Every year he seemed to increase by multiples. It was a good place. It was a comfortable place. But somewhere in his spirit he began to hear something calling him further to something much bigger. Something that would not leave him in a comfortable place for long.

He knew he didn't want to remain a salesman all his life. He dreaded the thought of trade shows and crude humor. He had always had something down deep inside yearning for more. Not necessarily more materially, though things are nice, but something that required more of him. He knew God had put more in him than this. He related well with Joseph in Egypt. He had learned to excel in every environment he found himself. Could this be his turn to be called out? Was God calling him to a higher place of authority?

Sitting in the *"Hot Seat"* Joel said, "I know it's going to sound strange, but I think I'm supposed to buy the company." We all looked a little surprised but not as surprised as Joel looked. He sat, slightly wringing his hands with a curious look on his face. He had already been contemplating the biggest questions. He didn't know how to buy a company. He didn't have the millions of dollars it would take to buy it. He didn't even know if the company was for sale. He wondered if he was even hearing God right. All of these questions meant that *"Hot Seat"* Prayer would be a good place to start. That night began a journey that would last three years.

Shortly after that Christmas Eve, Joel began to have the oddest occurrence every time he woke from sleep, was alone, or had quiet time to himself. The figure of $18 million would come to his mind. He didn't know what it meant or what it was for. Would he make $18 million dollars? Was he supposed to get $18 million dollars? In seemed relentless. It would happen at least two to three times a week. His only experience with something like this came as a boy while afraid a night. The countdown would begin in his mind, and he would race to get into bed before the countdown was over or death was imminent. But this was not like a childhood memory. It wasn't scary or worrisome. It was just there, in the quiet of his mind like a photo on a desk. You glance at it and then quickly forget and go on as usual. This went on for a couple of years.

Joel was in a unique position at ABG. He worked for this company as a salesperson for over a decade causing him to exceed the pay of even the owners. He had doubled the size of the company. As you can imagine, this was a cause for contention. Joel now carried power and influence making them uncomfortable to put it mildly.

The company was itself at a crossroads. The owner was in his eighties and in most points already retired. His son, an executive there, did not want to carry on the family business. The timing could not have been more ripe. This condition lasted two years. The $18 million dollar number continued to nag, and tensions continued to build.

The circumstance just emphasized what Joel believed God was telling him. He was indeed supposed to buy the company. He believed God. It might have seemed impossible. A pie in the sky idea. But it was real. And with God, all things are possible. He didn't know where the money was going to come from. He didn't know how much money he would need. He didn't have a clue about any of it. The only thing he did know was to start to figure it out. He knew if God was really calling him to buy this company, then God would help him figure it out.

He began to research by googling ways that people had bought companies. The internet was still young then which left him with many unanswered questions. He had to do a lot of networking to gain inside information related to purchases and how to raise capital and the structure of such deals. What kind of debt/equity would be needed? Who would even do that? How would he find investors? How does he retain control of the company with outside investors? How is it even possible to buy a $50 million dollar company with very little cash. He had to learn all of this and as fast as humanly possible. The timing was right, and it required starting now.

After a year of researching, Joel came to the conclusion that regardless how the deal shakes out, he must retain control of the company. If God wanted him to buy it, then He must also have plans for it. Without control, he would be limited with what he could do and how he could use it for the Lord.

He reached out to a family friend in Houston, Texas, who had sold a company to pick his brain and get advice. He introduced Joel to a man who was a private equity investor. This man helped Joel understand the inner workings of private equity and explained what to watch out for and what to look for in a partner. He spoke to a few attorneys who specialized in these kinds of deals. He spoke with my mother's then boss who was the president of a Fortune 500 company who was kind enough to give Joel an hour and good, sound advice.

The general consensus from all of them was do not give up control of the company if you don't have to. They told him to fight for everything he could, or they will take it otherwise. This only confirmed what Joel had already felt.

Just about the time that Joel had learned all he could, the owners of ABG fired their president and hired a consultant. As with most consultants, he was brought in to figure out what to do with the company. Joel and the consultant very quickly made a connection. They liked and respected each other's strengths. Intentionally, the consultant set up his desk next to Joel's to make it easy to get to know him. Regardless of the connection, Joel knew the consultant was brought in to figure out what to do with him. He was either a threat or an option. Like it or not, Joel was an integral part of any decision moving forward.

The consultant believed that there was something about Joel. He felt Joel could run the company though the owners weren't convinced. They decided to make Joel an offer where he would have a minority share of the company and based off performance and over time, he could gradually have more control. That's like offering a child one crayon out the large brand-new box. For Joel that was a hard no. Either he would buy this company or leave this company and start his own. He wasn't arrogant, just confident in what God had told him. As the whole scenario began to play out, Joel realized the $18 million number that kept coming to him was the purchase price even though they had not yet given him one.

Shortly after this exchange Joel sat in the consultant's office who was on the phone with the owner's son and blurted out that "Joel Luce wants to buy the company for $25 million dollars." Joel immediately said, "I didn't say that and that isn't what it's worth." They asked, "then what is it worth?" Joel told them maybe $21 million or less. Joel told me later that he was just talking in the moment. He was a good salesman after all. Joel had no intentions when going into the consultant's office that day. But the consultant wanted to move more quickly and help this process along. Within two days of that off the cuff conversation, the owner met with Joel. "What do you want to do and how are you going to raise the capital?" he asked. Joel told him "With private equity. And I'm ready to start."

Things began to happen quickly. Joel contracted with a broker dealer in May of 2006. They asked Joel how much money he could put together, and Joel told them one million dollars, even though we only had about four hundred thousand at that time. But with Joel's sales projection that year, he knew he would have the million in cash.

As the negotiations continued with the owners, Joel never forced the issue of the $18 million dollars. He never said, "I'll give you $18 million and not a penny more." He had kind of forgot about it as the process escalated. In fact, they all landed at $21 million which seemed a good deal to Joel, the owners and even the lenders and private equity thought so based off the huge response they received. Their agreement led to a signed letter of intent for $21 million dollars.

Throughout this whole process, we could see God's hand. It was like watching a master chess player. He was already thirty moves ahead knowing what his opponent would do next. Each person and decision were simply a move toward check mate and God wins again. The next move was one such move.

Strategically, the consultant pitched the idea to the owners that they should make Joel the CEO now and not wait. He wanted to keep the deal moving in a forward position and keep it from being able to go back to status quo. He wanted to leave no room for this deal to stall out. Both the owners and the consultant stood to win if they closed the deal. Of course, Joel loved this idea because it would enable him to control the company before he bought it and serve him well while presenting to investors, so he agreed.

Joel then put together a "book" and signed all legal documentation. He contracted with a broker who began contacting potential investors. They ended up with thirty possible capital sources. With good solid interest, they began the "road show" in September of 2006.

Joel did thirty presentations in three weeks. He began an exhausting but exhilarating whirlwind trip starting in Los Angeles, then onto Houston, New York, San Francisco, and then back home. He then went back to New York to talk again to a few parties who were very interested. Joel didn't care what kind of deal it was as long as he kept control.

He did five presentations in one day in New York City. While leaving one and running to another, one potential investor from Houston, whom he'd met the day before, called Joel and said, "what would it take to stop the road show, because we want to do the deal with you." But Joel knew for the long haul that he couldn't work with them, so he turned it down. At the end of the New York trip there was one group who was very interested in the deal, and they all seemed to hit it off except for one huge caveat. They wanted the majority stake. They would be putting in over $20 million compared to Joel's $1 million. They told him that no one would be willing to give him the majority ownership. *But God.*

About a week after the road show, a hedge fund out of San Francisco called. They said they wanted to do an all-debt deal. That would mean that Joel would retain 100% control even though he only put in $1 million dollars. The Chess Master calls "check." It seemed too good to be true. To make sure this was real, Joel and the brokers met with the hedge fund and looked at the term sheet. This was the last term sheet out of thirteen other offers of every kind to hit their desk. A billion-dollar hedge fund out of both New York and San Francisco wanted to put some money to work. The timing was perfect for a deal of the century. Joel would have the $20 million dollars in capital and retain 100% control. *Only God.*

He accepted their offer the end of October 2006. Up to December of that year the deal had been about the $21 million dollars. And then Joel remembered the $18 million. You could almost hear the dramatic DUH, DUH, DUH in the background. Like a rock in his stomach, he thought, "God are you saying I should buy this for $18 million and not $21 million?

In January of 2007, that knowledge weighed heavy on Joel's mind and the owner was getting cold feet. He had misunderstood a tax portion of the deal. This caused a huge problem. They realized how much money they were going to lose, and the deal was in danger of falling through. They figured out that they were set to lose $3 million dollars. The consultant told Joel that the owner won't take three million less." Joel said, "I'm not offering three million less." But the owner's argument was that he wouldn't be getting $21 million. He'd be getting $18 million because of the tax issue. Somehow, they expected Joel to get them $3 million more dollars while not changing their taxes which would happen if they received the $21 million. It seemed an impossible task.

Though this was exactly what God had told Joel, the owners were saying they won't do it. They had no solution and made it Joel's problem. If this deal was going to happen Joel would need to solve this problem. He knew this was his deal. This was his promise from the Lord. This was exactly what God had said three years earlier. The question was, how in the world can he make up the $3 million dollar gap and in such a way that both the owners and the tax man are happy.

With the investors adding pressure and the owners back peddling, all eyes were on Joel. That night before the meeting that would either close the deal or lose the deal, Joel came home loaded down with concern. He spoke to me about it and thought about it some more. He prayed about it and felt to look at all the details of the deal.

Late into the night, Joel scoured through all the paperwork and the many unique assets the company held. There was a million-dollar life insurance policy fund that paid out over a ten-year period to the widow of a deceased president of the company. There was a fund that paid for family education that was an asset of the company, holding approximately $400,000 dollars. There were also two other assets not used for the operations of the company. Their total came out to $3 million dollars. There it was in black and white. He'd found it. "Check and Mate!" Now he needed to see if the owners would accept his solution.

The next morning Joel came into the conference room where the owners and the consultant were all in a meeting. Everyone was sullen and upset because they assumed the deal was going to fall through at the eleventh hour. The consultant went with Joel into his office to explain how the owner was not going to budge. Joel interrupted him and said, "That's fine. Here's what I'm going to do." He then laid out the plan of the four different things that added to $3 million dollars. The purchase price would be $18 million not $21 but the owners would get their $21 million and retain their tax status. A deal that would even satisfy the IRS.

The consultant ran back into the meeting with the owners and told them Joel had the solution. The owner's son came running asking, "did you really solve it?" Joel explained it all to him and told him, "Now go convince your dad." He said he absolutely would. But Joel isn't one to wait around for others to decide his fate, so he interrupted their meeting himself and said, "do we have a deal or don't we?" As Joel looked around at all their smiling faces, the answer was obvious. The owner said, "Yep, we have a deal."

They closed Valentine's Day 2007, just one week later. And to add icing to this cake, the consultant gave his heart to the Lord and his life was radically changed. God was already using the company for His own purpose.

God's thoughts are higher than our thoughts and His ways are higher than our ways. His purposes and plans go beyond what we can think or imagine. Joel thought he needed experience, knowledge, and whole lot of money. He thought he needed the ability to make $3 million dollars appear out of thin air. But God would teach Joel that he didn't need money, or experience. He didn't need to be a miracle worker. He just needed to know that one that is. No matter how big your seemingly insurmountable mountain is, God is bigger. He does the impossible with just a word. And when He does it, even those around you will marvel. God will prove to you and all those watching that *you don't need money. You just need God.*

PLAY CALL: *Have faith and go.*

As a teenager I loved scavenger hunts. Each team is given a list of items they need to acquire to decipher and reach the destination determined by the planners of the scavenger hunt. When you start you don't have

what you need, and you don't know where you are going. We enjoy the surprise and mystique of it all. We
are confident we will find what we need and get where
we are going all with blind faith. But somehow in the
throes of life we forget to live with this childlike faith.
We get bogged down with fear not having what we need
and not knowing where we are going, so much so that
we often never start. You will never reach the heights or
go the lengths you were destined to if you don't believe
that God has a plan for your life and then get busy finding it. We have a limited amount of time on this earth.
Jesus said we must work while it is day because night
will come, and we will be out of time. Don't let doubt
and fear keep you from starting. I know the one who
planned your scavenger hunt and He's planned a destination that will blow your mind.

HAVE FAITH AND GO
It's All or Nothing

When our children were little, they never worried
about how things were provided for. If I told them to go
get dressed, that meant there were clothes already prepared and available for them to wear. If I told them to
go eat their breakfast. That meant that there was food
already available for them to eat. They simply needed
to go get it. Obedience to God is as simple as that. If He
has given you a task or instruction, all you need concern

yourself with is obeying. He has already made the provision for you.

Matthew 1:22 (NKJV) says, *"But be doers of the word, and not hearers only, deceiving yourselves."* Hearing God is a blessing, but it isn't the end. It's the beginning. We must do. It's in the doing that we see the miracles.

Many of the miracles of healing came with an instruction. Like, "go to the river and wash." "Show yourselves to the priest." "Take up your bed and walk." "Go and sin no more." "Remove the stone." The ten lepers Jesus healed were healed as they went. Your miracle of provision could be in the going and your obedience to the call. This is how my husband Joel received miracle provision and instruction. He just kept going. He started from where he was and followed each new step that presented itself. He didn't let what he didn't have stop him from going. He had everything he needed at the point that he needed it.

Matthew 17:24-27 (NIV) says,

> [24] *After Jesus and his disciples arrived in Capernaum, the collectors of the two-drachma temple tax came to Peter and asked, "Doesn't your teacher pay the temple tax?"* [25] *"Yes, he does," he replied. When Peter came into the house, Jesus was the first to speak. "What do you think, Simon?" he asked. "From whom do the kings of the earth collect duty*

and taxes—from their own children or from oth-
ers?" [26] *"From others," Peter answered. "Then the*
children are exempt," Jesus said to him. [27] *"But so*
that we may not cause offense, go to the lake and
throw out your line. Take the first fish you catch;
open its mouth and you will find a four-drachma
coin. Take it and give it to them for my tax and
yours."

The principles found in this passage will help you navigate your scavenger hunt with joy and not fear.

Principle 1: *Don't worry about what others expect.*

Peter was asked to pay a bill like everyone else. When Jesus heard this, he wanted to correct Peter's understanding of how the Kingdom works. Jesus clarifies that those who require the tax don't require it of their own children but from strangers. Jesus didn't want Peter to feel obligated to pay something he wasn't expected to pay. When you're in covenant with God and walking in obedience, He makes the provision. Jesus said in Matthew 11:29-30 (NKJV) 29 *"Take My yoke upon you and learn from Me, for I am gentle and lowly in heart, and you will find rest for your souls. 30 For My yoke is easy and My burden is light."*

People will try to put undue burdens and requirements on you. They may say things like, "you can't because you're too old or not old enough." "Why don't you do it like so and so?" "You're not qualified. You don't have a degree in that field." "You don't have the right connections." "You don't have the money." The list is literally endless.

Don't take their words to heart. Don't worry what they think about you or expect from you. They aren't the ones planning your destination nor are they the ones providing the means to get you there. If God said go, then go. He has already mapped a plan for you. Jeremiah 29:11 *"For I know the plans I have for you," declares the Lord, "plans to prosper you and not to harm you, plans to give you hope and a future"* (NIV).

Principle 2: *Go fishing.*

Jesus told Peter to go fishing. When we hear the term *gone fishing*, we think of rest and relaxation. And you should too. Jesus didn't tell Peter, "Well you'd better think of something." Jesus sent Peter on a fishing scavenger hunt. He gave him an enjoyable task. It was something Peter knew how to do very well. Peter was a fisherman. God is not going to tell you to do something you are not equipped to do. He knows you. He has a tailor-made plan for you. He literally gave Peter a step-by-step plan of what to do. *"Go to the lake and throw out your line. Take the first fish you catch; open its mouth and you will find a four-drachma coin. Take it and give it to them for my tax and yours*" (Matthew 17:27, NIV). Each next step was given so Peter would know what to do. The money wouldn't appear until he first went and followed the instruction to go. Following God's plan sets God's plan of provision in motion.

At each next juncture, the provision will be there, and you'll know what you are to do next. God isn't sending you on a wild goose chase. He's leading you somewhere. My mom used to tell us, "If you knew what God had for you, you'd want it." And she's right. Don't stop shy of attaining the prize. Paul said in 1 Corinthians 9:24 (NIV) "*Do you not know that in a race all the runners run, but only one gets the prize? Run in such a way as to get the prize.*" Win!

Principle 3: *Be the solution.*

With Jesus's instruction, Peter became the solution. Jesus didn't go fishing. He sent Peter. When my husband needed $3 million dollars for a tax issue, he became the solution. After prayer, the instruction from the Lord was to search through the paperwork, Joel found what he needed. Don't be frightened by the next need that presents itself. Jesus knows where the money is. It may be in the mouth of a fish or a pile of paperwork, but the provision is already there and the instructions for what to do with it.

Remember who you are. You are a child of the King. You are exempt from the worlds systems. We have the grand privilege of living by faith. We've the opportunity to be party to the impossible every day. Today, I hope you go fishing. I challenge you to go on the scavenger hunt of a lifetime and prove that You don't need money. You just need God.

PRAYER

Father today I thank you that I am your child. You have already planned a wonderful future for me. I thank you that you have already made provision and prepared me with all that I need to accomplish it. I know it's a good plan that is full of good things. Teach me to live in childlike faith. Strengthen me for quick obedience and fill me with your purpose. I declare and decree today that I am well able to possess my inheritance. In Jesus's name, Amen.

CHAPTER 15

The Conclusion of the Whole Matter

Jaime Luce

My mother sat on her couch in her usual place of study and began reading her Bible. Like so many times before, she came across a passage of scripture that grabbed her attention. She had just finished a grueling forty-day fast. As Zechariah 8:19 jumped off the page, she knew in her spirit that God would be calling her to several more fasts. But she took comfort knowing the result would produce joy and gladness. Though the thought of more fasting was not a pleasant one, her heart was always to honor God's words of instruction. Conquering a forty-day fast, coupled with the encouragement of knowing how it would turn out was the catalyst she needed during a time of great uncertainty for her, my dad, and our family. It would be six months after completing the last fast of that instruction that we all began to understand what the continual fasting was about.

My husband and I, our children, my parents, and my siblings and their children, had just made the change from our previous place of worship. Gathered around our kitchen table, we began to pray and ask the Lord for direction. We somehow felt that what would come next involved all of us. Phone calls began coming in from people asking us if we were starting a church, which was news to us. But with so many calls about the same thing we felt we needed to ask the Lord about it. From that time together, we decided to hold an "interest" meeting for all of those who continued to call.

What began as a single meeting quickly grew to a weekly Sunday evening meeting in our home. Doing it this way meant no one had to miss attending their own churches. The numbers of those attending continued to grow, and calls continued to come in. It seemed clear that God was birthing something. So, with the fear of God, we accepted the call.

On Easter 2006, we officially launched the church and held our first Sunday morning service in our home. We would clear out all the furniture every Sunday morning and set up chairs and a sound system. We used my daughter's bedroom as the nursery, our pool house for children's church and our pool for baptisms. We would project the worship songs onto the wall above the fireplace and had parking attendants help run people from the public parking areas to the house, complete with greeters and ushers. It was full blown church but in our house.

We were growing quickly and knew we couldn't remain in the house for long. In preparation we sowed for a harvest of a building and people. The church began tithing from all the tithes received and then gave out to five other ministries. We wanted to be blessed and be a blessing. My sister Jenny, who was a licensed real estate agent, along with my husband Joel, and my father Jim, began looking for property or a building for the church. They looked at every school, piece of property, and building in the city that could hold a growing church.

After looking at forty-four possibilities, we realized how difficult this was shaping up to be. Even when we would find a building, the zoning was an issue. The conditional use permits were impossible. The city made it very clear that they did not want any more churches in their town, and they said it right out. But we refused to quit. Then one day, Jenny felt to look again at a building that wasn't zoned for church use. As she read every detail of the building code, she came across what seemed to be a loophole we could jump through. It stated that if the tenants of the building used a certain percentage of their warehouse space to help with humanitarian efforts, they could then use 10,000 sq. ft. of the buildings space for worship services.

Well, that was all we needed. To us, it was the cloud the size of a man's hand. We jumped on that immediately. We had several non-profit organizations that we partnered with to help them warehouse their service goods and allow us worship space.

But the planning commission was determined to scare us off. Even though the property is surrounded by public parking, they refused to allow us use of it and said we would need to get conditional use permits that were written into the leases of the surrounding businesses. They thought we were dead in the water. We began seeking the help of our neighboring businesses. Four of them turned us down. We only had one final option. It was a family-owned business, and we hadn't heard back yet whether they would help. We knew it was asking a lot, to have them rewrite their leases to accommodate us. Most wouldn't want to go through the hassle.

We needed to plan for either possible answer. We decided to go get lunch at a nearby pizza place. As we were eating, that very family came in for lunch. They recognized my father and came to say hello. They inquired about how it was going and if anyone else was willing to help. We explained that they had all turned us down. Little did we know that our spur of the moment lunch was a God appointment.

After lunch that day, the father of that family called a meeting. He told his sons that he wasn't happy about how the city was treating a church. They voted that day to give us the easements. It was nothing short of a miracle. But that wasn't the end of the fight.

With all conditional use permits in hand, my sister Jenny, my husband Joel, and my father Jim went to the planning commission meeting. To our surprise, one of the neighboring businesses was there to fight against us using the building. He wanted to expand his current business and he wanted the building for himself. He began arguing and ranting so fiercely that it seemed a losing battle. But in the back of the room, Jenny quietly prayed in the spirit without stopping and suddenly the head of the commission stood up. Moments before, he made it clear they didn't want a church in that building, but with all the proper paperwork and documents ready he said, I guess we can't stop them, and permission to use was granted to us.

We wasted no time in getting the architect to draw up the plans for the budgeted build-out. We had already been having services in the house now for a year and the projected time frame to finish would be another year. We never dreamed that we would be holding church in our house for two years with over 100 attendees, but the people were so eager to serve that it made it all possible.

A contractor was hired, and we began construction. This presented a new possibility to the city. They may not have been able to stop us on the front end, but they weren't done trying on the back end. They began issuing fees meant to gouge us and hinder our budget. One fee alone was assessed at $64,000 to use the existing pipes for water usage that none of the surrounding buildings or previous tenants were asked to pay. What the city didn't know was that our attorney was the same attorney that had worked for them previously. With his help, we avoided being taxed in the way they'd hoped because we were a non-profit. God was definitely fighting battles on our behalf all along the way.

To fight in faith as a church, we had all the congregants who wanted to participate, come to the church while it was under construction, and we all began writing scriptures about what we were believing for and the promises of God, all over the ground and walls, while bathing it in prayer. In total we wrote over 700 scriptures on the foundation and walls of the church.

As the project continued, so did the city's fees. With every change they demanded, new plans had to be drawn up as well as the budget to pay for new drawings and changes. When construction was drawing to a close, we were faced with the deficit the city had caused. In order to pay our contractor, we now needed an additional $200,000. My dad was feeling the pressure and unsure of what to do.

At the same time, my husband Joel had planned a wonderful family vacation for us and our kids in Hawaii and decided to ask my parents to come with us since we were so close to finishing the church. It really was a dream vacation. We were having such a wonderful time, but Dad was struggling internally about everything back home. So, while we were there, he began praying and felt the Lord tell him to begin fasting. Even though he wanted to enjoy our vacation and the special meals we were having, he wasn't deterred. He began fasting while we were there. When it was time to come home, he hadn't received any instruction from the Lord except that he just felt to go see his tax accountant when we returned.

The first week home, Dad called a meeting with the church advisors. He explained where things were at and simply told them he was going to see the tax accountant. He was hoping the accountant would have some ideas. When Dad told them his plan, one of the men on the advisory board asked if he could go with him to see the accountant. Dad told him he could and gave him the details.

That same week they went to see the accountant. To my dad's dismay, he offered no solution or help. Then to my dad's surprise, the board member turned to my dad and said, "Well I've always wanted to do something big for God. Let's do this thing." He proceeded to write the church a personal loan. The Lord had shown us once again: *You don't need money. You just need God.*

From that moment on, the blessings began pouring in. One of the congregants called the church and asked if we needed any office furniture and office equipment.

He was closing a business down and needed to get rid of what he had. He literally supplied the church with desks, chairs, computers, phones systems, copy machines, and more. It was everything right down to paperclips. We became an instantly operating church office in twenty-four hours.

Multiple businesses then contacted us and began making donations. An ambulance company donated cribs, changing tables and supplies to furnish our nursery. A Christian school donated children's tables and chairs for the classrooms.

Then to add to an already miraculous start, one of the couples in our church asked to speak with my dad. They asked if we had priced how much carpet would cost. Dad told them we couldn't afford to buy carpet yet to which they replied, but how much do you think it would cost. When he told them how much it would be, they wrote a check to not only cover the carpet but to also purchase the material for the curtains and décor of the church.

The family of course made their own sacrifices, offerings, and purchases for the church as well. While the Lord blessed our personal business, we were able to purchase the sound system, leaving no need unmet. Everyone was so overjoyed at what God had done. He not only met the need of the $200,000 dollars for construction, but He also met every subsequent need we had.

It was just as Zechariah 8:19 said. Joyful and glad occasions were upon us. We celebrated that we serve a real and living God who is faithful to His word every time. There is no need too great or too small that he can't supply. The conclusion to the whole matter is this: You don't need money. You just need God.

PLAY CALL: *Repeat until complete.*

The original Ford Model T cars had to be cranked in order to start the engine. If you wanted to go anywhere, you needed to keep cranking until the motor started. Lawn mowers had a pully that you had to pull over and over to get them started. We understand this concept well. If I want to be a professional football player and I hire the best coach money can buy, I won't become a champion just because I hired a great coach. It will be my repeated training. If I determine I want to live healthier and become physically stronger and I join a gym, it won't be the membership that produces results. But if I repeat the action of weight resistance over and over again, I will begin to see and feel the results.

Repeating prayers or fasting more than once does not indicate failure. It depicts continual dependence. Hebrews 10:36 (NLT) *"Patient endurance is what you need now, so that you will continue to do God's will. Then you will receive all that he has promised."* Though there are times that we pray once or fast once, and we see the answer, there are also many times, that to obtain the promise in front of us, we must do what needs to be done many times over. Paul taught us in 1 Thessalonians 5:17 to pray without ceasing. Why would we need to continually pray? It isn't because God wasn't able to do it the first time. Sometimes the task ahead is so large, we must continually humble ourselves and rely on the one calling us to the task. He knows that the repetition will train us and prepare us for the promised answer. The bigger the task, the bigger the reliance.

In 1 Kings 18 we read how Elijah was going to pray for rain to end the drought. Big need. He sent his servant seven times to go look for rain. It wasn't until the seventh time that the answer came. If he had stopped after only one or two times, the catastrophic result would have been the death of countless people from starvation. The bigger the need the more imperative to not stop short.

Before our family began the process of starting a church, God called my mother to fast and then fast again and again. Even when the process was almost complete, God then spoke to my father to fast again and see it through to the end. Even Jesus himself repeated an act of healing in Mark 8:23-25 (NIV), *"23 He took the blind man by the hand and led him outside the village. When he had spit on the man's eyes and put his hands on him, Jesus asked, "Do you see anything?" 24 He looked up and said, "I see people; they look like trees walking around."* ²⁵*Once more Jesus put his hands on the man's eyes. Then his eyes were opened, his sight was restored, and he saw everything clear."*

If Jesus understood that sometimes repeating is necessary, we ought not be discouraged when we need to do the same. Instead, we should be encouraged that when it's all said and done, we will see everything clearly.

Principle 1: *Do it again and with all your heart.*

2 Kings 13:14-19 (NLT) tells us:

> ¹⁴*When Elisha was in his last illness, King Jehoash of Israel visited him and wept over him. "My father! My father! I see the chariots and charioteers of Israel!" he cried.* ¹⁵*Elisha told him, "Get a bow and some arrows." And the king did as he was told.* ¹⁶*Elisha told him, "Put your hand on the bow," and Elisha laid his own hands on the king's hands.* ¹⁷*Then he commanded, "Open that eastern window," and he opened it. Then he said, "Shoot!" So he shot an arrow. Elisha proclaimed, "This is the Lord's arrow, an arrow of victory over Aram, for you will completely conquer the Arameans at Aphek."* ¹⁸*Then he said, "Now pick up the other arrows and strike them against the ground." So the king picked them up and struck the ground three times.* ¹⁹*But the man of God was angry with him. "You should have struck*

*the ground five or six times!" he exclaimed. "Then
you would have beaten Aram until it was entirely
destroyed. Now you will be victorious only three
times."*

God wanted to answer the prayers of deliverance
for Israel and bring about a complete annihilation of
the enemy. He spoke by his prophet Elisha, giving him
their strategy for war and victory. Though King Jehoash
went to the right source and obeyed the prophets' instructions, he only did the minimum. His heart of surrender was not fully engaged. The prophet scolded him
and told him that his lack of fervor would mean only a
measure of success when God had intended continual
success.

Yes, it is imperative that we turn to the Lord. He is
the right source for our need. And it's as important to
carry out the instructions we have received. But it is
also important to stay engaged with a ready heart until
the thing is complete.

For my mother that meant fasting multiple times as
she was instructed. Had she thought that a forty day
fast should be sufficient, and that after all, Jesus didn't
do more than that, then we may never had been prepared for what was going to take place. And had my father not followed the instructions to fast again, we may

have won the victories up to that point but lost the subsequent final battle.

If you have ever tithed, but only a few times, you
may have never seen the harvest from your seed. That
is like planting a crop and trying to harvest too soon.
You run the risk of either killing the seed or harvesting
an undergrown and sickly crop. We tithe as a practice
in order to see a full and bountiful harvest. That is why
before even having a building; the church gave tithes to
other ministries as a regular practice. We were planting
a crop and expecting a ripe bounty.

Principle 2: *Don't be offended at God's instructions.*

> [1]*The king of Aram had great admiration for Naa-
> man, the commander of his army, because through
> him the Lord had given Aram great victories. But
> though Naaman was a mighty warrior, he suffered
> from leprosy.* [2]*At this time Aramean raiders had in-
> vaded the land of Israel, and among their captives
> was a young girl who had been given to Naaman's
> wife as a maid.* [3]*One day the girl said to her mis-
> tress, "I wish my master would go to see the prophet
> in Samaria. He would heal him of his leprosy."* [4]*So
> Naaman told the king what the young girl from Is-
> rael had said.* [5]*"Go and visit the prophet," the king
> of Aram told him. "I will send a letter of introduc-*

tion for you to take to the king of Israel." So Naaman started out, carrying as gifts 750 pounds of silver, 150 pounds of gold, and ten sets of clothing. ⁶The letter to the king of Israel said: "With this letter I present my servant Naaman. I want you to heal him of his leprosy." ⁷ When the king of Israel read the letter, he tore his clothes in dismay and said, "Am I God, that I can give life and take it away? Why is this man asking me to heal someone with leprosy? I can see that he's just trying to pick a fight with me." ⁸ But when Elisha, the man of God, heard that the king of Israel had torn his clothes in dismay, he sent this message to him: "Why are you so upset? Send Naaman to me, and he will learn that there is a true prophet here in Israel." ⁹ So Naaman went with his horses and chariots and waited at the door of Elisha's house. ¹⁰ But Elisha sent a messenger out to him with this message: "Go and wash yourself seven times in the Jordan River. Then your skin will be restored, and you will be healed of your leprosy." ¹¹ But Naaman became angry and stalked away. "I thought he would certainly come out to meet me!" he said. "I expected him to wave his hand over the leprosy and call on the name of the Lord his God and heal me! ¹² Aren't the rivers of Damascus, the Abana and the Pharpar, better than any of the rivers of Israel? Why shouldn't I wash in them and be healed?" So Naaman turned and went away in a *rage. [13] But his officers tried to reason with him and said, "Sir, if the prophet had told you to do something very difficult, wouldn't you have done it? So you should certainly obey him when he says simply, 'Go and wash and be cured!'" [14] So Naaman went down to the Jordan River and dipped himself seven times, as the man of God had instructed him. And his skin became as healthy as the skin of a young child, and he was healed!* 2 Kings 5:1-14 (NLT)

We may know exactly what our need is but not want to do what it takes to meet the need. We may get offended that God would ask us to do something that we don't want to do. We value our opinion more than the outcome. For example: Our church needed $200,000 dollars. My father could have been greatly offended that God wanted him to fast on his vacation. He may have reasoned that he may never be in Hawaii again. This may be his only chance to have this experience. Certainly, God wouldn't ask him to give that up. After all, Judy had fasted five different times already. There must be a different or better way to meet our need.

Had he thought that way he would have acted just as Naaman did. Naaman almost went away without a healing just because he didn't like the cure. But understanding that if we are never offended by God's instruction's, they will always lead to God's answers.

This same principle works with every circumstance whether financial or not. If I am offended that Luke 6:38 (NIV) says give first and then it will be given, then I forfeit the rest of the promise of the verse. The full promise says this, *"Give, and it will be given to you. A good measure, pressed down, shaken together and running over, will be poured into your lap. For with the measure you use, it will be measured to you."* I can't expect a bountiful measure unless I willingly bountifully gave. The measure we use will be the barometer of what we receive. Whether God asks me to fast over and over, or give over and over, I am not offended. I understand the heart of God and His desire is to answer my every need. He is not offended that I ask largely of Him, and I am not offended in the instruction He gives me. 1 John 5:3 tells us that His commandments are not burdensome. If I am willing to do what He asks of me, He is willing to bless me and give me victory over every enemy I face along the way.

When starting the church, we had many battles to overcome. So subsequently there were many arrows we needed to shoot to ensure our victories. You could say that we needed to dip seven times or look for rain until it arrived. One time wouldn't get it done. God had us on repeat. But God's strategies and instructions are always right and never offensive. He always has the right and good answer to any need we face.

In the end, it really boils down to this one understanding. The conclusion to whole matter is this. *You don't need money. You just need God.* He is the source and the supply. All that you will ever need is found in Him.

If you've been offended and realize that you were wrong and you want to make it right, you can do just as Naaman did and simply correct it. Go back to the Lord and ask for instructions. He hasn't changed His mind about you. His is no respecter of persons. If He still met Naaman's need He will still meet yours. Let Him give you your much needed instructions. Follow them as many times as necessary and watch God do the impossible for you.

PRAYER

Father, forgive me where I have doubted you or stopped short of your will. I determine today to follow your instructions because they are life and help to me and never burdensome. I will obey and keep obeying. I will give and keep giving so it can be given to me. Thank you for always loving me and always being ready and willing to meet my every need. You are my source and supply. I will listen to you with an eager and willing heart, knowing you will see me through to victory. And I will give you all the glory for the great things you have done. In Jesus's name, Amen.

Conclusion

Jaime Luce

Everything that we have written about in this book can just as easily be your story. God is no respecter of persons. If you will make God's ways, your ways, you will get what only God can give. Scripture is rich with instruction that leads to life and prosperity. Proverbs 9:10 (NKJV) says, *"the fear of the LORD is the beginning of wisdom, And the knowledge of the Holy One is understanding."* And in Proverbs 3:13-18 (NIV) we read, [13]*"Blessed are those who find wisdom, those who gain understanding,* [14]*for she is more profitable than silver and yields better returns than gold.* [15]*She is more precious than rubies; nothing you desire can compare with her.* [16]*Long life is in her right hand; in her left hand are riches and honor.* [17]*Her ways are pleasant ways, and all her paths are peace.* [18]*She is a tree of life to those who take hold of her; those who hold her fast will be blessed."* Did you catch that? Those who hold her fast "will" be blessed. Blessing naturally flows to those who exercise God's wisdom. The only effort we need to extend is obedience to the ways of God. Then you will reap God's rewards.

John tells us in John1:1-3 (NIV), *"In the beginning was the Word, and the Word was with God, and the Word was God. ² He was in the beginning with God. ³ All things were made through Him, and without Him nothing was made that was made."* He is the I am. Everything that is, came from His hands. He is the creator and the sustainer. James 2:17 (NIV), *"Every good gift and every perfect gift is from above, and comes down from the Father of lights, with whom there is no variation or shadow of turning."* God does not change. According to *Hebrews 13:8*, He is the same yesterday, today, and forever. How he feels about you is immovable. His ability to care for you never diminishes. All of creation displays his abundance and we live and benefit from its provision. Our part is to lay hold of it.

By putting God's word to work, you exercise your faith to receive what is supernatural. What is impossible with man is possible with God. *Luke 18:27* It doesn't matter how large the mountain of need is. The God who created the mountains can still move them. He is still parting sea's and still changing lives.

You know what you need to do. We have given you the tools or as we like to call them, play calls, and the biblical principles and strategies to do it. Our hope is that you've discovered the truth that you don't need money. You just need God. He is the giver and sustainer of life. Every need we will ever have, He is the supply. There is only one criterion to begin. You must have a personal relationship with Jesus Christ.

If you have already made Him your Lord, then just begin. Start with the first need you face right now. Take God's Word, apply the wisdom you have gained and by faith, believe you have received. Continue in the Word and in prayer for your direction and allow the Holy Spirit to guide you through the principles He gives. If God directs, it's a sure thing.

If, on the other hand, you have not surrendered your life to Christ, you can do that right now. You don't have to wait another minute. You can be washed clean from all sin and shame and given a brand-new clean slate. God wants to give you a fresh start that is free from the mistakes of yesterday. His word to you today is from Jeremiah 29:11 (NKJV), *"For I know the thoughts that I think toward you, says the Lord, thoughts of peace and not of evil, to give you a future and a hope."* You can live the life that God has dreamed for you. You can begin walking in the wisdom He has provided that will set your course for blessing. Once you have made the decision to follow Jesus Christ and live a surrendered life, everything will change. Scripture says in 2 Corinthians 5:17 (KJV), *"Therefore, if any man be in Christ, he is a new creature: old things are passed away; behold, all things are become new."* Then he says in John 10:10 (NKJV), *"The thief does not come except to steal, and to kill, and to destroy. I have come that they may have life, and that they may have it more abundantly."* If you want that abundant life, begin by saying this prayer:

Father, thank you for dying for me. Thank
you for making a way that I could live my
life in freedom from sin. Thank you that in
exchange for my broken life,
you provide a life of abundance. I recognize
that I need you.
I know that you want to supply all my needs.
I want to know you and your ways.
Fill me with your Holy Spirit. Guide my
thoughts and give me right desires.
Bring back to my remembrance your
principles
so I can walk this new life with you, under
your covering and in your blessings.
No matter what I need, I now know that
You're the answer.
I give you my heart and my life. Make me
a living testimony of your great mercy and
love.
Bless me so that I might be a blessing to others. And I will remind them that they don't
need money or any other thing. They just
need you.
And I will give you all the thanks and praise.
In Jesus's name, amen.

If you have received Jesus as your Lord and Savior, we'd love to know about it. And if you have applied the principles found in this book and have a testimony, please share it with us. You can email us at

mail@jaimeluce.com

If you prefer to mail by post, you can send it to
Jaime Luce Ministries
220 Newport Center Dr. #11-207
Newport Beach, CA 92660

We pray God's continued blessings on you as you live in accordance with His word. Remember, you don't need money. You just need God.

Judy Mercer is a seasoned speaker with years of experience teaching and mentoring the Body of Christ. As an inter-denominational Bible teacher and speaker for over forty-five years, she has ministered at churches, retreats, seminars, and Bible conferences. Judy also served in the marketplace. She retired after thirty years as the Executive Assistant to the President & CEO of a national publishing and communications company.

She lives with her husband Jim co-founded Connection Church in Corona, California, where they continue to serve.